THE PROPHET

Commentaries on Dead Ends and Other Perils

As Seen From a Jungian Perspective

Mitchell Ritter

COMMENTS FROM READERS

On Mr. Hide's Progress

"...a deep exploration of personal experience, self-evaluation, anger, discover, loss and love......though the details of the journey are not spelled out...the nature of the discovery process is clear.....The Seussian form is a delight. The problems we encounter in life - both physical and emotional - coupled with our own insecurities - forces us to deal with these hiccoughs as and when they occur with little or no reflection on the root causes. How we deal with them shapes our character to a certain extent but is that the real person? We do not have the reflection of hindsight to correct? "

"Questions, questions , questions?
Love - still an enigma?
The mystery of life still to explore?"

"The book stayed with me for days...."

On Six Years

"What a massive achievement............well done."

"I found the verse format both novel and absorbing, The content frank, insightful, sensitive, idealistic, erudite, all encompassing, analytical and poignant. You might wonder at the list of adjectives, but each one reflects a myriad of connecting thoughts so better to portray an assessment than a copious amount of verbiage. ..... uncertainties bubble to the top of the fast flowing river of life

On In the Seventh Year

"...observations carved out of current events, society in general or trends in our culture are filtered through the lens of European influenced psychology AND the rapid heartbeat of America. If you hunger for productive reflective, dive into his poetry and you will get plenty of food for thought."   "Rich and Compelling.....i strongly recommend this for anyone asking the questions "WHY" – or who have forgotten just how important that question is...."

"Until you make the unconscious conscious it will direct your life?

C.G. Jung

OTHER WORKS AVAILABLE BY THE AUTHOR

***MR. HIDE'S PROGRESS** – a short story about why people make the wrong choices, is available on

WWW.Amazon.com/mitcellritter/MRHIDESPROGRESS

www.createspace.com/**6876165**

***SIX YEARS – A CONCENTRATE OF LIFE** – the first phase of the author coming home after half a lifetime away

www.amazon.com/mitchell ritter/ebooks/SIX EARS

www.createspace.com/**6876165**

***IN THE 7TH YEAR – THE FUTURE IS WAITING–** Phase II and taking note of just how much American culture had moved on from the 1970's, is available on

www.Amazon.com/mitchellritter /INTHE7THYEAR

www.createspace.com/**7888004**

***THE PROPHET – Dead Ends and Other Perils** – A look at the road we are on, where it will take us from the heart,

www.amazon.com/mitchellritter/the **Prophet**

www.createspace.com/**7189577**

***AVAILABLE IN *EBOOK* OR SOFT COVER FORMATS**

Mr. Hide's Progress – A short story about why people make the wrong choices. A book about wanting change for oneself so much that love takes hold, providing the impetus. But there is always a line those desiring change must cross. To leave the familiar comfort of the past – no matter how much one may suffer from it or look into the unknown, and turn back.

Six Years – A Concentrate of Life – A collection of poetic reflections based on the authors return to his native New York City after 30 years abroad. Why poetry? Rather than put all his insights into a logical order according to his own outlook, the author offer up a "tappas" selection of 5 different themes we all share. So, if one day, some specific challenge calls for a fresh look, it should be readily found among the thirty plus poems included in this collection.

In The 7th Year – The Future is Waiting - After having made what he thought to be sufficient progress in understanding his own changes during his years in Europe, the author thought himself ready to enter the "implementation phase. What did he find?? A land which had abandoned the values he knew, only to embrace others. His challenge? To see if there was some point of intersection , broad enough for it to make sense to continue his road home.

The Prophet – Commentaries on Dead Ends – A series of reflections on the road this great nation is currently on. A multifaceted look at how we have changed as a people, what our new values are, have they cost us who we were, and will the road we are on take us to that destination we have forgotten how to imagine. Always there with the question "why," one is rarely left without some new perspective to consider in searching for answers to the questions we all face.

AUTHOR'S NOTE

Why Rhyme?

For those of you who have been intrigued by the cover imagery, somewhat less than inviting for some – and instead of finding a collection of political essays, but rather a collection of rhyming verse - read just a bit further before putting it down.

Poetry? Rhyme? That's for English majors, artsy people, children perhaps, and the overly subjective who write impenetrably personal lines. I used to think that too, though I was always a fan of Shakespeare and Dr. Seuss. At least until I started writing it myself.

How did that happen? Out of the blue. Simply stated, I found my prose (and I wrote a great deal professionally - and was told quite well) becoming professorial and so well structured that it didn't leave much room for surprise or dialogue. As people's inclination to take the time to read something of substance was declining, I realized I needed to reconsider.

Personally, I write to clarify my thinking, as having to put my thoughts to paper required passing them through a logical filter. The result was that I was writing more to convince than to engage. And in so doing, I realized that my writing was not helping me find answers to important questions that logic failed to provide? How is it that since most philosophers and intellectuals write in prose? They sought to erect a logical structured argument that was not designed or a dialogue. No one likes to be lectured at. convinced rather than challenged to think themselves, and particularly not now. And then it happened. A significant event in my personal life left me in a situation where my prose failed me. And this is how I discovered that prose is closed ended, with the conclusion being present before the discourse has occurred. In other words, we generally know where we will wind up before we begin. The journey is one of construction rather than discovery. Logic and structure dictate.

Poetry, on the other hand, obeys other Gods, most notably those deriving more specifically from emotion. Rhyming invokes the musicality of rhyming which cannot be squeezed into a logical structure. It must follow it's own course, and we must follow. But most of all, it is a matter of substance. Emotion brings the content, and it speaks a language that is metaphorical.

Two lines would come into my head, simple rhyming couplets of four lines each, and I was off, not knowing where I was going. The result is not devoid of logic. Rather, I think it is logic and emotion working together – as they should – to produce something far more creative and engaging, assuming one is so disposed. Prose is expository, unidirectional and generally less engaging. Poetry, or in my humble case, rhyming, is evocative, designed to affect rather than convince, and once entered its realm, doors open to another form of communication that can be far richer in terms of discovery than prose. This isn't a contest – both have their usefulness. But I did want to share with you how a non-poet discovered a very complementary means of written expression which has provided me with insights that I might not have discovered otherwise. Try it yourself, set free your emotions, put the demands of structure and logic aside, or a time at least, and follow. It's a wonderful mental vacation, and a chance to discover more about yourself than you might have imagined.

Without any claim to being a poet, I rhyme my way on this journey, and am grateful for the gift it represents. I offer it to you in all humility so that you can swallow your fear of looking ridiculous, and as they say in French, "…take your courage in both hands…," and set yourself free.

And finally, rhymes are not meant to be read like prose. I can't imagine anything more counterproductive than to read one poem after another.   Rather, these are appetizers, *tappas, "amuse-bouches,"* whose purpose is to open the appetite rather than close it. Let yourself pick one that calls out to you, take 5 minutes to read it, and then go off to whatever you had planned to do. If I'm right, as you digest it, some nourishment may take place, a seed might be planted, a new question might arise. And if it does, you might just come back for more.

FROM A MUCH VALUED FRIEND AND READER

For those who have read any of my previous work, there is a poem about '*Two Ladies*' who I met in Central Park, and who had the graciousness to befriend me, and later, my work. They are among my most sincere and authentic readers one can have, and often drop little pearls here and there which challenge me.   One day not long ago, in normal conversation, Carole quite spontaneously said to me "…You have a lot to say." Her tone betrayed nothing, and I spent a good part of the day wondering if she was teasing me or just speaking – as she and her friend Cindy often do – with the greatest of naturalness, ease and simplicity.   As often happens, I had to write something to think her comment through. I sent both Cindy and Carole the poem, entitled *"So Much To Say."* Here is what Carole wrote back. How lucky am I?

Read on and see for yourself…..

Mitch,

Great poem.

Feel assured that "What you have understood" does make perfect sense.

You **SHOULD** observe our world and comment (in poetry) on all you see.

You **DO** have a lot to say, and that is good. It is enlightening to those who read your work.

Also, Cindy and I want to thank you for your fantastic introduction of 2 mysterious ladies in the park.

You have a gift.
 Carole"

Carole Eisner
caroleeisner-sculpture.com
sculptor, mother grandmother and so much more

Cindy Gin
World traveler, mother, grandmother and someone who has embraced life in

her own very unique way."

INTRODUCTION

For those of you who have read my previous work, this could be considered the next stage of my return to the States. *"Six Years"* was a look inward to the new experiences I needed to reset my life after having spent 30 years in Europe. *"In the Seventh Year"* was supposed to recount my efforts at, rich from my experiences and insights, building a new life for myself in a place I thought I knew. Full of what I had learned about myself, it was time to test it against my environment. The experience was sobering as I had underestimated just how much had changed in the American psyche during my absence, and just how much of a different direction I had taken.

So how did a Brooklyn boy become a Prophet somewhere between his exile and his return home? So many factors influenced me, most notably my many years abroad, speaking other languages (I smile - when we refer to such as a "foreign" language, as if our mother tongue was natural and all others were foreign. That's quite an exercise in egocentrism in my view, and it's actually quite funny), having been married to a "foreigner" (to continue the amusing metaphor), raising two wonderful children, having lost too many dogs, having worked in so many different fields, and so on. But what changed the most for me was the realization of just how different we all are when it comes to our values, which we usually participate in rather than choose, and whose foundational assumptions are almost never question. Why? Because my own experience forced me to do just that. It was challenging, but not without its rewards. To speak another language, to live in a culture that is not originally one's own, to merge with people who have an entirely different set of basic assumptions and values, and perhaps most of all, who haven't known you or your family growing up, but who give you a second chance, an opportunity to discover who you are without the bonds of the past which will inevitably hold you back. To do all of this as part of a process of opening oneself to new possibilities and growth, and not to embrace uncritically the new culture, is perhaps a lot to accept. But if one can manage it, the result is a broadened perspective, an understanding of how many more questions, important questions, there are, than ready made, easy answers.

If this sounds presumptuous, the result has been just the opposite. Having been born and grown up in New York City, one cannot help feeling more worldly, more advanced, perhaps even smarter than others. My time away led me to fully understand just how little I knew, and didn't know it.

My return, as documented in my previous writings – both in prose and rhyme – has not been without challenges, for I now have two eyes to see with rather than just the one I had when I left. And as I love my country for what it represents, I have been deeply saddened by the road it has taken during my many years away, for we have lost touch with the central myths of our history. We have given in to prosperity, facility, avidity and have paid a heavy price. Jean Piaget, the famous Swiss cognitive psychologist, described the process as "decentralization." Simply stated, it is the growing awareness that we are not the center of everything, typical of young children, as we move towards a realization of our place in a larger existence. This allows children's intellectual development to go from magical thinking, to more concrete, experiential thinking, to the final stage of formal, or abstract, thinking – the ability to project oneself into another time or place, and anticipate without having to actually be physically present. It is the source of creative speculation, planning for the future, making good choices based on prior experience, and that "… it is not " *all about me.:*

Cognitive development is driven by many factors, many collective and external. And it can find itself reversed, though more on the collective rather than individual level. Progress does have its opposite, *regression*. Living in a place where the core value is success, itself defined by wealth, power and prestige, all imply competition. Once perhaps it was a matter of how one won. Now it is simple the fact of winning which counts. And to do that, the scope of acceptability, even if illicit, has widened considerably. The only exception – don't get caught (another lost value – ownership of one's mistakes).

The 2016 Presidential election was a shock to many, though for me, it was not a partisan defeat. Having grown up in New York City, the antics of our current president were well known, obvious, and worthy of ridicule – whatever his wealth. His values were transactional, self-serving and devoid of any self-awareness, humility or shame – the keys to wisdom. With a constant need for recognition, a compulsion to self-aggrandizement, a disregard for learning – all hallmarks of a classic narcissistic personality disorder – he is not the cause of our problems. Rather he is the symptom of a society which has gotten lost, embracing materialism as the antidote for an emotional vacuum, and infected with an avidity which can only lead to its eventual decline. Why? Because the problem is now cognitive.

Reality is a construct guided by our values. If these values are now driven by greed, avidity, alienation, egocentrism – that explains our vision of the world. Enough people subscribe to the values the president incarnates. Values can change based on experience, but more importantly, what is missing – the curiosity to reflect and not just react.. How can a nation make the right choices if it doesn't know who it is any longer, and contents itself to grasp at anything which might resemble an answer, or offer vacuous recipes for health prosperity and happiness. Life is challenging. That is why we grow. But if our purpose is to avoid difficulty, then what will become of us?

Prophets in the past have been clothed in divine inspiration. I have not that pretension. I care about the world, its marvelous creatures, the promise we represented once upon a time. What values will we have left to guide our children through the inevitable challenges waiting for them? Prophets see things differently having a perspective different from the mainstream. They have no need to be right or wrong, only heard. For theirs is a warning of what might come to pass. Ignore it as it rarely comes in an engaging form. But then my point will be proven. Blindness is a disease of the mind as much as the eye.

And finally, remember the promise every parent should make in their heart. That we will leave a better world than the one we were born into. Are we on the right path? Your answer comes with profound consequences. Use your mind – not your brain to look broadly, think largely, inclusively, for we can only sink or swim together.

"It all depends on how we look at things and not how they are in themselves"

C.G. Jung

THE POEMS

THE PROPHET

October 2017

As I mentioned previously, the working title of this collection was The Prophet. Why? Because, without any effort or pretension, I tend to see things differently than most. I think I've been on this path for a very long time, always searching for the essence of things, the fundamental explanations, the ones which can answer not just the how but the why. Some find me interesting because of it. Others advise to dial it down as conviction and a different perspective can bring conflict, even in the best of circumstances. Perhaps there's also a bit of Don Quixote in me. Whatever it is, I can't not be who I am. Perhaps in reading further, you may recognize that I am mistaken. That perhaps I am not as alone as I think. That would be excellent new indeed.

Who is a prophet but a man apart?

Not belonging to any group at the start

He sees the world through a different lens

An alternate vision of the future he sends

His focus differs in one fundamental way

He looks to the future and not the next day

No visionary in the traditional sense

No business goal nor innovation in the present tense

He sees what's wrong, when others see what's right

Why focus on what's working, how is that worth a fight?

The tone is moral, or so it sounds

An air of certainty often abounds

Yet none are plagued more by doubt

Though sure of his vision, there are few supporters about

For the prophet exists to give voice to the question

To derange, to provoke, to challenge complacent digestion

He arises in times when the mind is in retreat

When appetites prevail, and not just to eat

When time has shrunk and the future dissolves

When all that counts is me, around me all else revolves

Lonely is the prophet – written with a small "p"

No great man in history will he ever be

His life is no example of how others should live

He is ordinary in most things, yet he needs to give

Life has chosen him, made him self-aware

And most of all, has taught him that one must care

There are days when life fills his chest with cheer

Embracing, engaging, not inhabited by fear

Recognition in the form of having been heard

Gives wings to his step, though he be no bird

His values are few and humanly clear

Walking his line, trying to stay near

But focus such as this comes with a flaw

His vision neglects the rest of the draw

For this line is by definition with the rest out of synch

The wind may fill his sails, but the boat may still sink

When the light meets the darkness which surrounds us all

Those who stand up and resist its call

Are brought to ground not by anything of note

Betrayal won't keep for long any vessel afloat

To date we've believed in the cycle of things

As night follows day, and as night day brings

In days of disappointment, one comes to doubt

Has the wind shifted so much the boat can't come about?

So here we are, back where we began

I know what I will do, perhaps more than most any man

Clarity helps to stay the course

At times it weighs heavliy on any horse

Once seen, however, one cannot deviate

So it is for the prophet, such is his fate.

Why is it he has no choice?

For rare are those who hear The Voice

Considered many explanations though none suffice

I think he is indeed chosen to be Nature's device

SO MUCH TO SAY

December 2017

It has occurred to me on many occasions that who am I to write and publish so many poems. I did it first for myself to find plausible answers to the events and motivations I observed around me. I was still unsure if this was not some exercise of hubris. But then, my two ladies, whom I've mentioned previously, came to my rescue once again. They are possessed of the wisdom that only some women can possess – something so natural as to not be denatured by analysis or critical thinking. They speak with no malice, nor pretense, nor need to express anything but the essential question too often forgotten by others, but rarely by them.

Two ladies I know, walking in the Park

I look forward to meeting them for they brighten the dark

I share with them my poems, which they generously read

And their words of sincerity I always heed

One day, with no malice, after a flurry of verse

One of the ladies asked me, for better or worse

"Who knew you had so much to say"

I had never thought about this before that day

And with a smile at the simplicity and the truth it spoke

I asked myself the question, was I smart or just broke?

The answer came to me quickly, though I knew it long before

Observations, not judgements, are a mirror hung on a door

Offered for free, worth only what benefit they may contain

A beam of light or a permanent stain

But to live in blindness, with nothing seen

No matter how sharp one's vision, or intelligence keen

So engaged in life, for our world to care

There is so much wrong, one must dare

To point it out, to speak up when seen

To protest against that which is small, backward and mean

For the world belongs to all of us together

No more to one or another, regardless the place or the weather

And insofar as I continue to believe this is so

I will share what I see, always eager to know

If what I have understood makes any sense

Or if my fellow humans have grown simply too dense

To see the obvious, to understand

Should we fail to care for what is ours, we might lose this land.

AWARE

November 2017

This one is a bit embarrassing for it started out rather focused, with a simple message – get your noses out of your phones (have you noticed many have dropped the "smart" – a hopeful sign for me as they have contributed to making us dumb). But as I wrote, more and more thoughts came into my mind pointing to things we have lost awareness of. Is this so grave? It's a definite trend. From productivity to convenience, on to distraction and finally to isolation. And sure, it's a long poem, but there's a point there too. We are in such a hurry that we can only become superficial, never giving ourselves the time to fully digest, critique, supplement and finally refine whatever it is which requires our attention. And taken together, we just grow ever more lazy, self-absorbed, and living in the present only.

As you walk down the street do you stare?

At the passersby? Do you notice? Do you care?

Absorbed in your thoughts, who knows where

Or do you look to see, aware?

Of those whose paths you daily cross

Blinded by their insignificance, you're the boss

What of these others sharing your space?

In some unexplained hurry, a race

Are they too living in that place?

Where passersby have no face

The silence fills your head as it seems to grow

Our surroundings we no longer care to know

For have we grown to a such a degree

There is little else that we can see

My needs, my wants, my desires are all that count

To a point where all the others to very little amount

Rich from a vision so distorted, we no longer see

That we all share the same reality

But our need for importance so great has grown

It's now surpasses all that we've known

Like some hungry beast than can never be sated

No concern for the future, however ill fated

If I must go up, the rest must descend

So inflated, yet so vulnerable, at all costs defend

So far so good, until a challenge is met

My native superiority, is it such a sure bet?

My confidence must reign, though built on sand

That shifts in reaction to the subterranean land

And should it fail to pass the test?

Ending up second, third or even fourth best

What then? Who am I? All is called into question

As I attempt to reconcile reality with my self-perception

A challenge, nowadays, few care to meet

Fantasy the more comfortable choice, with rationalizations replete

So there we have it, the only choice we ever need make

Do I truly care to live in the real? Would it be a mistake?

And if I have been taught how to sustain a lie

A significant amount of time I might buy

Dire warnings may come, of how this will end

Who is this voice such a negative message to send?

How can they be sure, how can they know?

If I want it thus, then it must be so

I assume the folly has now grown clear

If I choose fantasy, it's reality I fear

And with each step back into fantasyland

That place where I can only win – no need to take a stand

Where my life can appear successful, even grand

Yet why do things go wrong? I never understand

When truth dissolves into the sand

One must wonder – was it all thusly planned?

The new world we walk in

Assaulted by the ever present din

Noises aplenty, yet bearing no name

Flatten our world, making it all seem the same

What of the topography of our lives?

Those little things for which one strives

The choices we make

The things we take

They make us who we are

Are they made to take us far?

But if these differences we dismiss

So focused on our personal bliss

Yet we've forgotten the debit side of the equation

Hail to consumer, the indebted nation

What has been lost?

What is the cost?

Has there descended a wintery frost?

Or into an unrecognized inferno tossed?

Have we all thus accepted to be?

Have we closed our eyes, thinking we still see?

Twofold would by my reply

And here is the reason why

For some things we need the world inside

Limitless, from the laws of physics one need not abide

But before we can take such a leap

A promise to ourselves we must keep

Withdraw we may from the world outside

For never was it meant to be a place to hide

But rather when the question we ask

Has life become too big a task?

When the physical world with its limits

Our imagination it inhibits

Turn inwards from whence we came

And find the original source and our true name

Once freed from the constraints of reality

Our vision can see to infinity

This is where we can go to reflect

To know if our road needs a redirect

The second piece we risk losing

Comes from how we do our choosing

For reasons exist which we prefer to ignore

Yet there they are, not behind some secret door

Therein lies a treasure trove of memories forgotten

More often than not, misbegotten

Hidden perhaps yet nonetheless they toil

The more we resist, the more they boil

Defining the imperatives we will not see

That's how they control our destiny

With words like love and need and ambition

A shorthanded language is now our new tradition

Reduced to some vague vernacular

Deprived of their meaning by some cultural Dracula

Who sucks the life instead of making sense

With no nightfall to call him hence

For these things we so readily subsume

Having taken up residence on the moon

Ignore this fact, emotion drives every choice

Its words may be different, but not its voice

Anger speaks to confuse

Seeking only to light the fuse

To stir things into a state of confusion

Till we see no truth, only dark illusion

I want this more than that other thing

It's this one, not that one, who should be our king

Songs will be written, crowds will sing

At the coronation, bells will ring

They've joined their hearts to this thing they won't explain

All countervailing forces bend, now seen with disdain

Though far afield have I strayed

The message, I hope, has stayed

Rambled a bit, to what end

To force reflection, time to spend

When we rush ahead, nothing deeply is understood

Ignorance wears a cowl, and a hood

The light cannot penetrate

Stupidity breeds only hate

Close or open will it be, the gate?

That will determine our collective fate

For Life is varied, its differences, infinite

Simplifying what we see, can only limit

Growth recedes if the world we shrink

And with it the boat we all share can only sink

CLOSING DOORS FIRST

July 2017

Though this rhyme is told in the first person, it is not my story. And for that I am grateful. Though, having to set off on my own early in life, I saw many who never managed to do just that. And the price they paid was high. Here are some thoughts on how and why it happens.

We seem to believe the future waits through an open door

As if all we need do for a world that offers more

But who thinks of what we've brought in that bag?

It's the past still on our backs, creating a drag

It's filled with images of varied hew

Different places, different times, some old, some new

Loaded down, we bend under its weight

Somehow unaware of its influence on our fate

The voices, the images received mostly from others

Provided our first impressions from fathers and
mothers

Like a rough sketch, to be completed later on

We're building the foundation our lives will rest upon

Unnoticed by most who labor for years

One theme recurring, and it's the mother of all fears

This is the gift that keeps on giving, if we allow

Each new field approached requiring a plough

Of rocks and stones we thought it cleared

Nor ready for planting we saw as we neared

We'd closed our eyes to just what we feared

Too often that happens, strange, even weird

Molded we are by messages shared along the way

We try not to listen to what they say

Slowly but surely, these wise words sink in

We think they are gone, but they whisper in the din

Telling us of all that we cannot do

As if hidden in these words they somehow knew

With but a small drop of poison, the toxin can spread

So when we look for our courage, we find doubt instead

With each recurrence of this sort

Projects grow always more easier to abort

Faith flounders, our vision less clear

As time moves on, no great adventure for us – we'd rather stay near

To home, that place that's safe and secure

It holds us close as if to ensure

A future where risk has no place

As we start to grow lazy and sit out the race

And then it hits, one day a light breaks through

Notice the high walls now blocking the view

A lock on the door, though it's always ajar

But to walk through it to freedom seems just too far

My fortress, once where I knew no fear

Has become a prison, unmistakably clear

If this is so, and now I am less young

Do I still have a chance or has my song by another been sung?

The door is open, the gate is down

Yet there I remain sitting, wearing a frown

In comes fantasy to save the day

I can mix and match the facts any old way

To hide what's real, the better to conceal

And most of all, the pain never to feel

How did this happen? Did I ever have a choice?

Of course, but they were always there, in muffled voice

Sending me an image not of how I could be

They sent me an image of what they wanted to see

In word benign, words full of praise

As if my self esteem to raise

But I always knew, somehow hollow it rang

Even unspoken, another's praises they sang

I had no idea of my capacities for real

It seemed at times that self esteem was a steal

A bargain, a discount, a knockoff or sorts

And on that beautiful clear skin now I saw warts

Here I sit, my feet stuck in cement

Nothing do I own, for I dared only rent

Though there always remains that same choice

If only I dared to set free my voice

To walk through that door and close it behind

To see the world through my own eyes, and the others,
never mind.

DISTRACTION

December 2017

Here's a theme I've been harping on for a long time, though I don't think I ever came at it from this angle. Slipping in between Aware and Authenticity seemed an appropriate place. In essence, I've often said that when the future of this era is written, should we survive as sentient beings, Steve Jobs will be considered the anti-Christ for having offered up the culture of distraction. Originally it was hidden under the guise of productivity, and maybe that was even his original intent. But something led him to direct the potential and the fun of a user friendly computer to an ecosystem whose goal was more fun and distraction than towards anything truly productive. Up there in the Pantheon of modern day anti-heros would also figure Mark Zuckerberg – Lucifer himself. I haven't written a poem about him yet – perhaps another time.

The end of year is fast arriving

People in the city are still striving

Whatever field may occupy their days

Stranger indeed have become their ways

Something started awhile ago

Exactly when it's hard to know

Somewhere where the lines did cross

When distraction won and productivity lost

When technology enabled me to select

What I wanted and could expect

No care for those in power

Dictating what was offered from some high tower

From choosing music to the news

Rock, country western, jazz or the blues

Posting pictures of how busy I was

Updating constantly – oh, the buzz

Liking, friending, sharing and more

Living life like this could never be a bore

At first it was amazing to be in control

Filling my head to the brim of the bowl

But then a strange thing happened, I failed to see

Everything had now become all about me

The limits of my world began to shrink

I could pick my information and have no need to think

A universe composed by me for me alone

Even texting replace speaking on the phone

Certitude came by excluding any contradiction

For advertisers our preferences made easy their predictions

Why bother looking to things that were new?

When I'd narrowed it all down to just a few

But something seems oddly off

Living in an echo chamber – you might scoff

It's true, this *"all about me thing"*

It's not so great to feel like a king

For my realm is small, boring at best

Can a mind grow again?– I'm tired from distraction, I need a rest?

For all this control distracts me from another fact

When I leave my head, I'm no longer sure how to act

Was this the plan all along?

Start me off with choosing a song

To slowly sink in a world of me

How does that make anyone free?

All this noise, activity galore

How quickly did we become a bore?

Distraction – Job's gift to humanity

Enabled our move to inanity

For distracted means I'm not paying heed

To what's really important and what we need

Having no time to think or plan ahead

Deep inside seems to be dead

Maybe we'll grow tired of our own new state

And put some real food finally on my plate.

AUTHENTICITY

November 2017

I've often thought about what quality makes the most sense, is the most central, even at times drawing others to them with no intent to form a clique. Quite the opposite, for while putting forth a point of view for others to embrace, there is no desire to be followed. The much maligned altruism? Irrelevant these days when everything is transactional. No, it's something more profound, coming from the depths of what we used to refer to as our soul (perhaps another anachronism in the ages of Artificial Intelligence). Listen, really listen instead of looking for an opening to kidnap the conversation. Their stories, or just their everyday conversation, and perhaps by negative example, one realizes that authenticity is not a state, or even a necessarily natural process. Rather, it is the consequence of a certain awakening that there are things larger than ourselves and our preoccupations, and that some of these things may be important enough to defend, even at some personal cost. It is a road one chooses to travel – at times challenging, at others rewarding. But in the end, as Jung said: "The greatest privilege in life is to become oneself." I would add that it is also perhaps the greatest responsibility, for if we take another route, how will we ever know who we are?.

There was time when it was a goal

To find one's path and become whole

Not selfishly, for to be is to share

Daring to live this way, one must to care

What is this thing authenticity?

Yet another word we use with little rigor or clarity

It implies some ideal, a trait in others we claim to admire

Bringing wisdom and peace, a steady flame, no raging fire

Some think it comes by itself over time

Requiring little effort, this path of mine

Acquiring the nutrients so as to grow

And in so doing, we shall all come to know

The secrets of life, the mysteries of love

To be filled with whatever allows to rise above

But life is not meant to work this way

Little peace, mostly turmoil, fills our day

Busyness squeezes out reflection and thought

Things, not wisdom nor peace are bought

As one by one, or many together fall

Who will remain standing, strong and tall?

Were there ever many who by example could show the way?

Who knew also to listen and not run away?

Who saw the value of time, why it was so?

What comes too quickly cannot prosper and grow

Into something of depth and vision long

And bind us all to creation, to which we belong

So put aside the distractions, hear the voice

Know that thoughtful silence alone can bring choice

To discern right and wrong as the mist starts to lift

And see how together good and evil knit

The fabric of our lives, the choices we make

Whether to give, or rather to take

For right and wrong are born of a moral thought

Of necessity, of good and evil were they taught

The former we create as we live and learn

The latter is innate, unconsidered, waiting not its turn

It is our beginning when there was no need to discern

Of it is our story written – rape, pillage and burn

It recurs of necessity, civilizations churn

To care, transformative, we must learn

To look up at the sky, not just the ground below

Goodness is a seed that upwards must grow

Until awareness dawns and we realize

Not every act deserves a prize

What we need, what we want – two different things

Consciousness lifts us up as if on wings

To see a picture more complete

With pros and cons aplenty and replete

To come together, stronger to be

Survival comes that way in fact more easily

With numbers growing, strength does too

Too easy it becomes to prey on the few

Whose voice bring us together as one?

What is not mine must be taken from someone

Willingly given? – unlikely so

And that's how we come to know

To know is to choose

If one wins, the other must lose

Do we delegate how we define?

When – if ever – should we cross the line?

Where, but more importantly whose guide to follow?

To know deep inside, instead from another to borrow

Beware the collective mind

Justification it can always find

Right or wrong are too often redefined

Cut loose from its foundations, it can be redesigned

And when that happens, and no one speaks

Out of the woodwork come the freaks

Those who have hidden awaiting their chance

To change the music and impose their dance

How the multitudes seem to enter a trance

Watch the goose steppers as they prance

What to do when one sees beyond tomorrow?

When it is still time to prevent the sorrow

Stand up and speak your mind?

Or join the others and sign

These are the moments authentic and real

When there is no choice since only right one can feel

To deny this truth would be oneself to deny

By this a soul must live or it will die

CARING – DARING

November 2017

Perhaps an appropriate poem to follow 'Authenticity" for it raises the fundamental issue of our emotions and the role they should play in the world. Sadly there has been a shift away from caring – currently more frequently used as a defensive term, as in "I don't care,"r than in the affirmative. But if we cease caring about anything but ourselves, then that which binds us to everything dissolves. Replacing feeling – now more associated with physical sensations, with material possessions, engages us in an endless succession of "more." Yet what we fail to realize is that this is a race we can never win, for even if we have enough money, we will surely run out of time.

A new kind of threat has arrived

From my logical side it is derived

After a pause new subjects more actua;l

Emotion looks at them – counterfactual

Perhaps that's when reason intervenes

When the threat is too close that's what it means

So here goes, a brand new start

And I will try to play my part

Of late hurt has entered my mind

I've let others in and seen how unkind

How thoughtless, taking all I can give

With nary a thought to how others live

For sure to survive, I can make it on my own

Though to do so my own heart I must disown

For I look at the world through eyes of care

And my values require I try to be fair

Knowing our views are not all the same

Mine derive from a different game

For I have lived in a different place

So many years, and they've left a trace

No better in one place than another

For each may from insularity suffer

But having two places, something new to synthesize

Gives depth to reality, as one begins to realize

I've come to think of this as a gift

But now I see it has created a rift

Are we meant to have but one point of view?

To stick to it fiercely, not to renew

To question what is held as the truth, one and only

To think in a place such as this, must be lonely

But it allows the suspension of thought

A collective mind this way is bought

This way there is no necessity

To test one's assumptions veracity

Where did it go, the desire to know?

What happened to the need to grow?

That which resides as potential, waiting to be fed

Yet if starved, it will soon be dead

So I look around, engage all comers

Open my mind, my heart, winters as summers

This is the right thing, so says my heart

Live your way, play your part

I've found a partial truth living this way

I listen, I care, I dare each day

But in return, like a thirsty man lost in the dunes

Only mirages dance for I meet too few moons

So here it is, my current conclusion

Our kind rates reality poorly when compared to illusion

For what's missing is most certainly what's felt

In the heart, not our pants, can we truly melt?

Starved of caring, we've tightened our belt

Indeed a weak hand ourselves have we dealt

Material goods have come to fill the void

Their pursuit helps the pain to avoid

Bluster, bragging, bullying gain

Showing off only serves to hide the pain

It's a call, in fact, that no one hears

Fear of being hurt has grown over the years

The years pass as our hunger grows

Much talk takes place yet no one knows

Theories abound, we embrace only the new

Where once there was water, there remains only the
dew

This I know so here I will say

Sooner or later there will come a day

When the hunger will deprive us of our need to feel

And reality will have extinguished our ability to heal

Artificial this, virtual that

The old fashioned things, if not forgotten, are not old hat

Our roots start to shrivel from lack of use

There remains no engine – only the caboose

For the longer we wait, the more we get lost

Am I alone in this world to see the cost?

WHAT HAPPENED?

January 2017

I had spent the day with a good friend who had gone through a recent breakup. We spoke in some depth of what happened, but more importantly, why it happened. . And how was it possible we didn't see it coming when the inevitability of it was clear? Who hasn't been there? Here's a few thoughts as to why there is always a "why," if only we have the courage to see reality rather than color it to suit our desires.

There are days, I'm sure we all know them well

When it seems we need another trip to the well

The one we count on to never run dry

Have you asked yourself if it could happen and why?

This well, a source, where you were born

Runs without pause, generous, our lives adorn

Like the blood that keeps us alive

Without it none could survive

We say it's the heart its residence

However improbable, it can make sense

In fact, how did this come to be

But a simple pump, obviously

Nonetheless, it can be broken

When hurtful words are too easily spoken

No link exists between heart and ears

Yet somewhere in between reside the fears

Who can among us can fail to recall?

The happy time before the fall

When all was good, no obstacle withstood

Whatever kept things as they should

The power flowing from this bond

It seemed they grew ever more fond

Every day it seemed there was the sun

Though the clouds soon followed on the run

Something was wrong, though what could it be?

Who knew on this day we were to be set free?

In a flash, everything changed

One's life forever deranged

A hole appeared deep inside

There was no escape nor place to hide

Alone in a way that resists description

Yet unmistakenly questions one's disposition

Happy before, carefree now

To continue alone, but how?

The days that follow seem obscure

No appetite for life, how to endure?

No other there to reassure

Of what in the world can one be sure?

Love is the mystery if seen that way

Who hasn't tried to explain how its wages pay

And blind, so blind, how could one fail to see

After all, every river flows in to the sea

I think there are answers, though they come too late

This failure to see lives within us, and counts not on fate

Our road traveled, if one cares to look

Could so easily be written in a book

The narrative, if not straight, at least unique

To look back to the past, it will always speak

Of mistakes that were made, that weren't mistakes

Words spoken with sincerity, or were they fakes

Promises made destined to be broken

Truths always present but remaining unspoken

Fantasy rules when all else fails

One by one, each spouse bails

Perhaps not gone, their body still there

What's left, however, was the care

Keeping the shame going, don't' rock the boat

Yet ever deep grows the moat

When is the right time to lance the boil

When did love start to resemble toil

When did one's courage abandon this home

When did you realize just how alone

The head has its reasons, cold and clear

Rooted in no emotion they know no fear

But the heart is the one to suffer, despising to live alone

Better to learn from the pain than simply atone

The lesson is simple, yet among the hardest to learn

When things fall apart and tempers start to burn

That is the time to raise the sheet

Take a stand, bear the heat

It will burn away all that's impure

The hurt will fade, confidence more sure

Broken hearts always heal

As long as one remembers always to feel

VOICES, CHOICES - From the "Chris Chonicles"

December 2017

For those of you who have been reading my previous work, you will be familiar with this series, which discusses a young man I befriended some 3 years ago. This poem relates my perception of what was going on with him as he struggles against elemental forces within himself, trying to free himself from his very considerable demons. This particular poem came after yet another failure in his attempt to stake a claim in this reality rather than the alternate one which has been his protector in times past, and has now become his jailor. I reflect on the extent of my commitment, why I made that commitment, and just how far it can remain useful for him, and not negative for me. Even people with deeply rooted psychological issues have a choice. , though in our blameless society this is not current thinking. They may lack the objective or financial means and even the motivation. But there is always a choice. If one abandons this perspective, attributing everything to illness, doors that might be available are not seen, or if they are, they appear closed. If this is what happens, any hope for the individual disappears. Without choice, there is no hope, and without hope, there can be no future. It can stand alone, but to get the full measure of just what an injustice Life has visited upon this young man, going back to the earlier poems would surely fill out the picture. I may publish a collection of all the poems I have written under th title " The Chris Chronicles," to include as well a more detailed explanation (in prose) of just what happened to him

The latest in a friendship whose purpose was real

To free this young man and let him feel

Free from the burdens of the past

So he can imagine a future of his own at last

Three years now friends we have been

Good things were done, but there was more sin

To test me, to see if I could be trusted

Often forgetting the times when he had been busted

For all things flowed in one direction

He had never learned to think otherwise in his reflection

So what has been my role these past 3 years?

To offer him a light at the end of the tunnel, free from his fears

For born into a world where no one cared

Survival assured only to those who dared

So he split in two, one on the inside, the other outside

His real self buried deep within where safely he could hide

This worked for a time as his world crumbled around

Constantly shifting, on the run, this was his ground

Now in his thirties with nothing of his own

Like an orphaned child by some wild wind blown

Never able to stay for long

He never knew what it meant to belong

But here is the challenge Life has sent his way

This friendship offers him a chance to stay

To stop running, always looking over his shoulder

A fantasy had developed, giving him a purpose bolder

Intelligence forces all arrayed to follow him always

Wherever he went, during his nights or days

Acquaintances conveniently speculated that he was mad

Paranoia. How simple it is to put on a label. So sad

But he was not sick, only wounded deep

For I could silence the Voices and him safely keep

The one inside who longed to be free

If the Voices could be silenced and he could see

Just who he was, and why he was an outcast

That if he could take one side, there was to be hope at last

I watched him struggle, saw all the signs

As his trust would grow and he crossed a few lines

Suddenly his face would grow dark

His friendly voice turned into a bark

He'd pick a fight, a victim once more

Better to run away than wait to be shown the door

That's how they worked, these Voices who once protected

Having outlived their usefulness, all help was redirected

They would not allow him to break their hold

Though over time, he had become more daring, more bold

He knows now that he must choose a team

To let go of the past which has grown mean

Like some fierce dog who fears all it sees

To fight to the death, never go down on its knees

So single-minded, allowing no thought

Rule number one – safety – in this net is he caught

I can only imagine the courage required

To free himself from this conundrum in which he is mired

To fire the one who has kept him safe

From the time he was small, barely a waif

But this is the challenge Life has sent his way

Choose he must, out loud he must say

"Goodbye old friend, I will never forget

But a new course without you I must now set

In a well deserved retirement you always stay near

Yet free me you must from this constant fear

For if you refuse to abandon your task

What from Life can I possibly ask?"

Emprisoned, outcast, alone with no hope

In these conditions who could ever cope?

Unknown is what the response will be

The Voices will not go quietly

They can make him mad, his security to ensure

Though I doubt the solitude he could endure

Or worse yet, no door, no exit is to be found

Neither forward nor backward, a ship run aground

I fear he would say *"enough," "there is now way ahead"*

The obvious answer, always present, he'd rather be dead

I don't know if he can ever be free

But in his life – and in mine – there is a role to be

We began something so fundamental in his life

Beyond any conventional role of father, brother, or wife

I am the anchor in reality, the ally who will not desist

His Voices hold fast, their grip unrelenting, continue to resist

I did not dream this would come to be my role

Though from the start, I saw in his heart a hole

So big, so wide, so much pain

Could whatever I have to show him wash away the stain?

And now, though his presence can weigh heavily

He has entered the tunnel and a light he can see

I cannot abandon him, though such might be my desire

For unknowingly, I have lit a sacred fire

Life betrayed this child by the place it reserved for him

He deserved not the fate, committed no original sin

So like it or not, I will see this through

And hope that he can manage – somehow – a life that's new

One where there is a difference between night and day

And without those Voices, he can have in his life a say

A CHILD OF NEGLECT

From the Chris Chronicles

December 2017

A reflection on the three years I have known Chris, of the insights I have tried to bring to him believing, and hoping, that somehow his mind thusly reinforced, might defeat his inner demons. Slowly a realization has taken shape in my mind, and a sad one it is, that I will not be able to do this for him, though I'm sure we both wish it could be so. He takes a few steps forward only to run away when the prospect of stepping out of his conundrum of a life gets too close. In spite of this, there is at times progress. Yet his demons refuse to let him go. But I've come to believe that, for him to find himself a path that can bring him some way out of his loneliness, the support I provide has to cease. I've observed myself as closely as I've observed him. And I marvel at how whatever it is that guides me, for it has long ago passed the stage where who I am has replaced what I do for him, seems to know the way forward for us both. Does that mean he will ever escape his personal hell? I don't know for at least I gave him evidence that someone could actually care for him. And that gave him a bit more courage to continue struggling. For Chris, life is and has always been about survival – not living. I cannot imagine how exhausted he must be caught in a life and death struggle with himself every hour of every day. I say this with deep regret for he never asked to be born, to be so unloved that in a moment of cruel clarity, he said to me "…I am so afraid of dying alone." A former mentor of mine, a man of little sensibility but deep intuition referred to people such as Chris "…These are the leftovers of God's anger." How cruel. How true.

How to hope when no love ever filled his life?

That he might have dreamed of a home and a wife

But none of that for him was reserved

A fate so empty that none deserved

Yet there it is, I have done more than my share

To right the wrong, I can no longer care

Something has changed, I know it's so

Now he must decide himself if he is to grow

So many things he never learned

So many times has he been burned

The world he knows is unique to him

No friend, no money, no family, no kin

Forgotten by all, alone his pride remains

Yet all that he has is covered with stains

Even as a child, seeking but to be known

Dismissed by his parents, abandoned to the wind, to be blown

To whomever felt a twinge of his pain

A welcome, a meal, some place for a time to remain

Yet always he knew the time would again come

Before being asked to leave, and be on the run

"Can I help? What can I do?

Anything at all. Can't I stay too?"

Perverse fate it, for the ground was prepared

He never believed he could stay, so he despaired

Turning hopelessness into destructive desire

Before leaving, at least break something or set it on fire

Settling the account before the meal can to an end

He was sent away, fences each time harder to mend

So has he lived these many years

Pursued by imaginary forces, the fruit of his fears

Wishing he could but not know how to atone

His greatest fear, I heard him say, is to die alone.

Who can't feel this deepest of holes?

How can a child such as he pay all of the tolls?

Back from the Hades he's never escaped

I fear for him the future he's shaped

One hope remains, that age may fill his empty heart

That once he can some day cease living apart.

ENGAGEMENT

OCTOBER 2017

One day last Spring, for no apparent reason, I had an altercation with a good friend of mine. It was pointless, but obviously I had unknowingly stuck my finger into some trape I did not recognize. He had reacted so violently, I began questioning others if they – as we all have – encountered such a phenomenon. Now clearly, my "intuition" knew before I did what would annoy him. Towards what end? I think during this period, I was frustrated with the lack of "caring" demonstrated by most people at all levels of conversation. I had grown tired of asking people how they were, and getting served a double helping of them, with no thought of how I might be. Seizing on this opening, it became something of a test. My friend unloaded on me, well beyond the scope othe situation, which also was of interest. I spoke to a common friend, and she explained it all in one word. Apparently, contrary to most, who prefer to remain behind self-protective walls, I engage with people.   Who wants to live in a prison, for that's what fortresses – appropriate perhaps at some time – ultimately become. Fortunately, and perhaps in part due to the friendship, I was rewarded with a positive outcome . The next day, my friend had resolved his anger, though he didn't share the source of it, and came to meet me in Central Park as we do every day, even offering his version of an apology. I was impressed. Not knowing if I had some responsibility in the altercation, I couldn't substantively apologize myself.   But I'm sure we will have more opportunities where I too can benefit by apologizing. Intuition is indeed a funny thing. And so are we,

What does it mean to engage?

Has it become so rare that it can enrage?

Or frighten to the point of flight?

Or worse yet, to start a fight?

After all, is it not what we desire?

To feel the closeness and warmth from the fire

Something can come along and change the tone

Unsuspecting, both erupt and in the end they are alone

I've seen it often, someone feels a threat

It can come from an old wound, unhealed as yet

An insecurity, a slilght, not intended by perceived

No one can be sure how their words will be received

But I have a gift of sorts that hones in on these sores

No longer by chance – accidents like my heart abhors

So gently I tread, feeling my way

Sensing when the ground is prepared, and I can say

First by Intimation, then more clearly still

My goal, to create a space tht's safe, quite and still

For a time I succeed, calming the talk

Yet sooner or later, the other will balk

For in addition to that which we say

 We are seen often in another way

 Not as we see ourselves, how could that be?

 No two pair of eyes share the same vision of reality

 It's odd how growing up we were often told

 Be honest, be yourself, be real, be bold

 Yet in the world of today is that still the case?

 I find these things have gone missing from most others
  face

 A mask is more malleable, easy to change

 Dialing it down, so as less to derange

Like some product destined for a wide distribution

Keep what you really think hidden in a diluted

Perhaps that's why, when so deprived

Our true selves rebel, if they have at all surived

It begins with disagreement, escalating fast

Becoming a battle of who will have the world last

No matter the subject under debate

Peace dissolves quickly and turns – for a time – into hate

So there we are, what to do?

It seems those preoccupied with this matter are just too few

Getting along should always be

If not the number one, at least the number 2 priority

But not at all costs, since cost there must be

Better to know beforehand it will not be free

Just keep your eye open – see early the signs

Consult both of you two minds

One to engage and stand your ground

The other to withdraw if in time one's place one has
found

In such cases, one can always choose

If it's worth it a friend to keep or lose

FRUSTRATION

November 2017

One year after the last election, my attention was drawn to the unmistakable fact that as a culture, as a people, we have ceased our march, however imperfect, towards progress, exchanging it for the metaphorical "good old days." I wondered what drives the reversal which finds its manifestations in all aspects of life: the retreat from connection, self-awareness, knowledge, curiosity, empathy. A long list indeed. To be replaced by a self-centeredness more characteristic of teenagers, a shift in values from the spiritual (i.e. not religious) to the concrete, the present overwhelming the remnants of the future, and the hope it engenders. And most strikingly to my mind, problems are no longer to be understood and resolved. Someone just needs to see themselves as "ill," or having some "disease," albeit vaguely, quantitatively defined, and a pre-packaged treatment or program, including pharmaceuticals, is offered as the solution. How does that address which faculty most ensures our species survival? The abiity to adapt to change is central. But if we choose not to understand the origins of our problems – or prefer to deny them, fail to anticipate consequences of our actions beyond the immediate present,, concern ourselves only with ourselves thereby ignoring our collective interdependence. Further we have come to delegate, or perhaps abdicate is a more precise descriptive, the solution to short-term oriented politicians who are more a symptom than a cause of our current ills. When a people fails to recognize its role in keeping a society collaborative, healthy and progressive on every level, there seems little chance of any long term success. We are defined by the responsibilities we assume as parents, voters, members of the larger group which alone can ensure our survival. The good old days, for those who knew them, were never that good. There were times of global war, economic dislocation, racial tensions, generational conflicts. Time knows but one direction. By wishing to contravene that constant, we are placing ourselves at odds with reality. Perhaps the period we have known, defined by progress in the form of distraction and convenience rather than any significant societal evolution, has returned us to a stage of psychological development defined by regression from adulthood back to adolescence. Is that what the people longing for the good old days really mean?.

Frustration could be a nation

A place to live in starvation

Not for food or water or even riches

But a place of ruts and muddy ditches

Not dug for any purpose real

With any source where one can heal

It is a place where choices earlier made

Deprives one's needs, fullness forbade

Nor is it a home of some static state

Where things level out and one can stay late

For it has a partner that emerges from behind

With an all too clear direction in mind

Let's say it starts somewhere in between

Where normal lives and can be seen

Yet when frustrations builds and desire is foiled

The waters grow turgid, agitated and roiled

The energy unleashed is of a negative kind

Downward towards darkness goes the regessive mind

What once looked sane, even innocent

Starts to resemble something bent

Where affection was once its goal, to share the time

It's now a matter of yours or mine

To give devolves into take

What once was real now becomes fak

Fantasy replaces what used to be real

Emotions vanish, what point is there really to feel?

So each withdraws to a safer place

Putting on a mask to save face

Such is the slope so many follow

Where fullness is traded in for hollow

The endpoint being a connection lost

And with it brings, alone the cost.

If any of this rings a bell

If you've been living in some sort of vague hell

The fog is lifted, clarity arrives

Make your choice – we don't get that many lives.

Reverse course – yes you can

No matter if a woman or man

Courage found, vulnerability revealed

Speak and listen and be healed.

THE COMPROMISE

January 2017

Who hasn't found themselves confronted with a choice, for after all, it always comes down to that. Two opposing forces with different points of view, different goals, yet forced by circumstance to live or work together? Compromise is a fact of existence. But in the end, it all comes down to just how much it costs, and something too often forgotten, what part of oneself has one abandoned? Too often, it's a piece of ourselves, and a necessary piece, we have abandoned, or just as bad, chosen not to defend. Not in the sense of being obtuse or doctrinaire, or needing to win at all costs. But rather when we must consider what's at stake, who will win or lose, and who pays the price. Somethings are worth the price, though at the time, we may think so. Just remember, there is always a choice if you have kept your voice. And must there always be a winner and a loser?

When it feels like life's roads are blocked

Doors that should be open are tightly locked

For reasons too harsh to recall

What to do so as not to lose it all?

A compromise, the space in between

Safe and risky, nice and mean

A no man's land one hope's to find

A place providing some peace of mind

A detour around an immovable "NO"

To that place we believe we must go

The goal is right, never lost from sight

A safe passage to avoid a fight?

But something happens on the way

The goal has a toll to pay

Remolded by the compromise

In shape, dimension, even size

Has it changed fundamentally?

Can it still make us free?

Or has something uninvited

The goal now different, somehow blighted

No heed is paid to its new form

As it is , becoming the new norm

And over time, if life continues thus

Why question it, why make a fuss?

But something else has taken place

When first embraced, to save face

We paid a price in courage then

Not strong enough to fight back when

The truth we could save

If only at that time we were brave

But putting off what must be done

To a later time, convinced the game still can be won

There's a time for patience, waiting for the moment opportune

The stars aligned favorably, the Sun and the Moon

Once Fate might allow such a day

Twice and begins a price to pay

But now that time has long since passed

A new way forward, another dye is cast

Courage, the victim of this deal

With a binding contract our fate we seal

Slowly, surely, our direction is changed

Options denied, life deranged

This path that we now tread

Could lead us to new life or to a place of dread

No longer free as we once were

Old protections gone, to this compromise the must defer

New rules appear, unsuspected

What lay written in small print went undetected

This place we chose because secure

Was never so, they are impure

Growth is blocked, our way clear no more

Once open to us, we face a closed door

The compromise, once hero of the day

The bill arrives bringing with it the price to pay

Thus are made futures unplanned

They come with their own demand

Time now to look back to the place and time

When we thought this way would be fine

If wise, we pause to see just the cost

And with it what we really lost

This contract, written perhaps in haste

The misperceptions and the waste

A road we thought was meant to be

Its misdirections we can now clearly see

Where courage was in short supply

Now's comes the time to ask why

Why continue down a road that's wrong

 Can we find our way back to a better song?

 One I still can recognize, warm and friendly

 One sung again in the key of me

 It can be done, chase away the craven words

 It's doves we need, not angry birds

 Know now compromise flows from fantasy

 The mind's playground, not reality

 As tempting as some sugar high

 Beware if that's what you choose to buy

Bend perspective from truth and reality recedes

And along with it, so too will true desires and needs

Help arrives once it's clear how this came to be

Pointing the way back to me

The road ahead can open, and call out to me

To resume my way, and more clearly see

How fear worked in silence to make me blind

Leading me astray, clouding my mind

Knowing now when to heed its voice

And when I always have a choice

COMPLEX EQUATIONS, SIMPLE MATH

November 2017

They say at man's plans God laughs. Add to that the unlimited complexities of individuals, multiply that by the numbers in a family, then add on to that a partner, possibly children, even pets, why not? What do we have? An equation beyond our ability to control in any way. So what to do? The only thing one can do is to find a means of understanding oneself, since it the only part of the equation one can, to some degree, control. An argument for self-awareness? That shouldn't be necessary, but there it is. Without it, one thing is clear. You are not driving the car. Some stranger with unknown motives is holding the wheel. Engage them. Find out what's on their mind. Make friends. That way, you don't have to be afraid of driving (a thinly veiled metaphor for Life, just in case). Just one thing more. This isn't a story for children where do the right thing and you get your reward. In this case, the reward is something even better. You get to be yourself.

Since my return fifteen years ago

I thought for sure that I would know

My path ahead, the life I would lead

No doubt guided my every deed

Though I have built a life of which I can't complain

Somehow fate seems my plans to disdain

Each initiative taken, though objectively right

Has sooner or later dissolved into the night

I went from confident optimism to something less

Darker days descended at times, I confess

But I am of a nature cheerful, in touch

If something is missing, I don't fret too much

Naively confident in what might wait around the bend

Life, after all, can be a generous friend

But one thing has remained beyond my reach

And though I help others, revealing rather than teach

I've passed through the gardens of blind youthful hope

It worked for a few years and allowed me to cope

But it brought no result of any duration

What else can grow but disappointment and frustration?

I tended to believe trust was not an issue of mine

After all, all alone I was fine

Yet with the years passing I came to realize

The obvious fact I'd been missing – regardless how wise

For marked by life's betrayals are we all, to some degree

We can compartmentalize, rationalize, deny – none of which will set us free

Born of betrayal comes a simple rule

In navigating life it has become the essential tool

Wounded once, wary always

And so we pass too many wasted days

Whether present in our minds or not

It lives in the shadows where it an safely ro

Afraid of being hurt if you let someone in

Self-protection the blessing? Openness the sin?

Unaware, the walls grow high

Before too long we no longer see the sky

Others may choose this path, , it will not be my fate

I know now clearly this is no way to find a friend or mate

I've staked out a middle ground, and defined its terms

No more fortified walls, moats or berms

With the years I've learned what was my share

No more projects demanding too much care

With no will to truly grow

This we all should come to know

Own yourself, be clear of debts

Open your eyes, stop with the foolish bets

Help transforms to neediness

The promises of change are worthless

Watershed moments exist in life too

Decision points where one can choose old or new

The truth reveals itself, there is no mistake

Stepping into the unknown, with the past, break

When standing on the line, look into their eyes

All will become clear – the truth or the lies

If more promises are offered, they're not ready yet

Time to pick up your chips and place elsewhere your bet

Each one of us an equation of complexity immense

Surrounded by a cloud of our own making, both thick
and dense

What we see may appear to be real

Though it hides more than it dare reveal

With as many layers as an onion peel

So many layers working to distort what they feel

Each of us a challenge, a riddle to solve

Ignore it and into confusion dissolve

Chemistry is Nature's way to attract

It lights a fire, and we react

Mistaking forces coming deep within

That are mostly superficial and very thin

We can know why if only we look

Some self-awareness, and maybe help from a good book

Chemistry is about reactions, two things coming
 together

More often than not, the union of elements is like the
changing weather

It can be cold or hot, calm or storm

Much of it influenced by the prevailing norm

But if you have learned from life and have fed your mind

The choice is clear – are the best choices the ones you've
  made blind?

If it's love you seek, first start with word

Do you want a base creature or a soaring bird?

And if so, why then, what are its traits

Does it seek only survival or lifelong mates?

Ask then what might be required, what qualities to find

That's it, start thinking, forget your brain, use your mind

Kindness, caring, loyalty and trust

It may be less hot, but comes with less chance of a bust

Now comes the hard part, I've avoided it until now

Take a good look at yourself in the mirror, and ask
  yourself how

How have things gone in the past

Have any of your previous unions been able to last?

And if the answer is a resounding no.

It's down that path you need to go.

Be fair. Be honest. If not you're not just a cheat

You're the victim too, and that's hard to beat

We think mostly of our wants, only to take

Did y ou ever consider that might be a mistake?

What does it mean to be that hungry and in need?

It means mostly that your values are based on greed

So the story begins not with what's wrong with the
  others

Nor is the most important part about your very own
druthers

It starts with the person you are and what you have to
  give

That's what you need to know before together with
 another you can live

Once that is clear, take a look around

Have you realized you've changed, not lost but found

Now you have it, your part of the equation

Ready at last to search by other means than temptation

It won't be easy, we control but half

And never forget at yourself and your foibles to laugh

And maybe hearing the laughter, someone might notice you

That's how it starts, into one from two

"The greatest privilege in life is to become oneself."

C.G. Jung

OUT IN FRONT

August 2017

A somewhat lengthy digression on how my life has taken shape, and the very active role I have tried to play in seeing things clearly and with purpose. So many of our decisions are made based on very little – mood, chemistry, etc. –but rarely with purpose. How does this happen? When we start delegating the central task that is becoming ourselves growing into responsible adults in the broadest sense of the term, when our perspective becomes so inward looking, when we lose the ability to empathize with another person, when the outside world overwhelms the inner world – all of these factors impede our development to the point where we often regress to some adolescent stage. And here, on my return to the States, I was struck by how all of these things were happening at the same time. Responsibility is the antithetical to entitlement. And owning them is the key to owning ourselves.

Much of my life has been subject to thought

Growing up in a time when that's what was taught

To consider who I was to become

Without arrogance, but to grow into someone

To see who myself was at a moment in time

To stay my course always, on the road that was mine

It has been a journey full of difference and discovery

And has preserved me from setbacks, often providing a
 rapid recovery

Like some multi-branched tree, life offers many choices

And one is subject throughout to many other voices

How does one choose the right way ahead?

The answer is never singular, never spoken, nor said

Among these many offshoots, so confusing at first

There are few that lead to good, more go to the worst

I believe this has been the sum of my wages paid

I have navigated my river and at times was waylaid

Never did I feel completely stuck

Nor ever did I seek to pass the buck

Unlike so many who grew up in my time and since then

To start with my own actions, transcribed by my pen

Neither to glorify nor to find an excuse

Only what falls under my control that's of any use

Mistakes are the bricks of the most solid kind

When owned by a responsible mind

Yet, finding another to bear the blame

Has become the new name of the game

The consequences of this are too many to list

Yet the result for us all is too clear to be missed

If no blame I accept for the poor choices I've made

If my soul is so fragile that the truth is forbade

I have chosen to be of no significance as I roam through my life

Fearful of all things, yet forbidden a knife

To defend myself against whatever threatens

No real control, my existence deadens

Any chance of seeing what my choice has done

Life is now lived only on the surface, all hot, now and fun

But what if my actions are of no consequence?

The sole impact of my passage her lies only in the present tense

Objects alone are now the measure of any success

What of my feelings? Abandoned, for they cause too much stress

Yet without them how is value apportioned out?

With no emotion invested, nothing holds any clout

One dreams not of that which might last

Without realizing it's the future that is now the outcast

Life grows boring – how often this word is these days spoken?

What it really means is that life is broken

Feeling is that which makes things important – more or less

And allows us to say clearly either no or yes

But if we've avoided such engagement with the world we live in

Or delegate our choices to any passing whim

How can that reflect how we really feel?

And what might make our lives the least bit real?

Embrace your emotions, reflect on them too

Life takes on texture, perspective and each day can look new

For they are the key to connecting with it all

And open the door to Life – no matter how big or small

No promise of success is therein contained

No life is ever completely ordained

I've lived my life in this way trained

Pushing back the limits, no borders by others framed

It has made me myself, he who owns his life

If tranquil is not the word, then neither is strife

Yet one downside I have found

In truth I did not see it coming, making no sound

On the matter of being only few to live this way

How to explain to those who chose not to stay?

Yes to this singular journey into worlds outside and in

Most have chosen alone the former sin

I find myself now, in the autumn of my time

Too often alone to see things thusly, and it's not really fine

But if whatever I have found is worth the value I see

Then is paying some price not a necessity?

There's a concept we too rarely critique

Is life really a commerce? Let's take a peek

Where did this come from, who takes the credit?

For the life of me I've no idea – so perhaps should we edit?

Yet without the balance it implies

With what to replace it?- More nonsense and lies?

It's but a rationalization so we can find sense where none exists

And perhaps the reason lies in something so simple the signals are mixed

We all begin life very much the same

Though infinite potential resides – neither wild nor tame

That's when the world steps in and the exchange begins

Battered we are by losses, raised up by wins

I discovered my strengths in leaving home

To a place where I was not known

I found I was not who I'd been told

In so doing I have become surer, more bold

Not only when from home, far away

Where family voices told me to stay

In a place they had defined

Not realizing just how I was undermined

Words spoken as if from love

Often hiding a vulture disguised as a dove

Demons passed on from generations lost

Though weakened by time, they still with a cost

No need for boasting, their voices now secondary

I discovered what was important. most of all to me

Unencumbered by concerns that were not mine

I run my race out in front according to my own time.

Out in front because few hindrances remain

Washed out of the fabric, like an unwelcome stain

Delivered from the burden placed upon me

I see the past as it was, and that makes me free

No blame to family or others to assign

To be from past errors, they must first be mine

To embrace the wrongs I have done

That's how the war can be finally won.

PART II

A NAME. A FLOWER.

November 2017

More grieving for Lily. The more I think about it, after 3 years and it is still fresh, I have come to a certain understanding of my pain. There has always been a sense of right and wrong deeply imbedded in me which has become more rooted in my soul as the years pass. Lily was only 8 when she fell ill for no reason one could attribute to her. She had all the qualities present in dogs – I know, another crazy dog person – and which are so lacking in ourselves. And her being taken from me, from the world, shook me to my core because it called into question my fundamental sense of justice, or in this case, injustice. It was my job to protect her, and though I did everything possible – and some would say more – in four months of living in hope when there was none to have, she was taken. And she was not taken gently for she basically starved to death, slowly, cruelly, and without any reason other than some random infection which destroyed her kidneys. Her last night, when she lacked the strength to get off the bed, she nevertheless went for a short walk with me. Each step broke my heart for I knew it was her last night. I awoke around 2, though I was more dozing than sleeping, hearing her labored breathing. I held her in my arms, reassuring her, as if I could stop her being taken. It lasted for awhile until I saw Death – much as we imagine him to be, a wraith-like insubstantial presence. He floated into the bedroom and I held her all the more closely. He saw me but said nothing. Her breathing grew more labored, and I said "NO" one last time. But it was too late. Death sucked the life out of her, and it was not easy. I thought for a moment to smother her with a pillow to speed her passage, but I lacked the courage. And so I thanked her for trying these past four difficult months, for she did it for me, and I told her she could go now. And she was gone. It was perhaps the worst experience of my life, and for this reason, and for Lily, I will never forget her.

How is it, a name, a flower?

Can retain such power

When it no longer lives among us

Something deeper causes the fuss

No obsession of loved ones lost

No accounting of any financial cost

Love and admiration know no bounds

Though they come from men or hounds

I thought the pain was slipping away

It did not visit each and every day

But I heard a tale of another's woe

The wounded heart again did show

The story spoke of premature twins

Born too soon to be met with grins

From the moment they were to arrive

It was a constant struggle to keep them alive

A boy, a girl, two fathers a brother
A family different, unlike any other
Two careers, families apart
Indeed these lives would fill any cart

These men stood guard as real men do
Though the final outcome no one knew
Their strength, their love, their fatherly devotion
They would have crossed any ocean

But humankind has no arms to fight the wraith
Neither black magic nor any faith
He comes when he does with no explanation
He lives apart from any nation

To suck the life, or is it our soul

He heeds no prayers having but one goal

The boy died in one father's arms

No amulets, no potions, no technical charms

There is some grace in such an end

Enough threads are left, their hearts to mend

The boy who left this vale of tears

I hope never knew of mortal fears

Some say to heaven he rose

An angel perhaps, who knows?

Gracious God kept the girl alive

To battle on, her fathers strive

Life and Death, I've seen both sides

One is everywhere, the other hides

When a life is given for us to care

Something special happens, and we dare

To believe that we can protect against all things dark

Such is our sacred charge, a holy mark

Hubris perhaps, a silly belief

Whatever happens, we will provide relief

Grateful should we be to dwell in a land

Where we are all powerful, wielding our mighty hand

Until the moment when from beneath our feet

The floor is ripped out, and Death we meet

He has no face, no substance, ethereal yet there

He has no emotion, he does not care

Bereft, powerless, all we can do is hold fast

Until the final breath is surrendered to Him at last

I'd never felt an emptiness like this

As the life was removed, in its place an ice cold kiss

My only solace, all that remains

Beyond the anguish and the pains

Is the dignity of the one so cruelly taken

In the face of it, by her I was never forsaken

She stayed for me as long as she could

The final days in pain, perhaps longer than she should

Selfishly I held her, I didn't want to let her go

Until the very end, I refused to know

So this is why, when a life is wrongly taken

We feel so very deeply shaken

For the silent oath never to fail

Is broken, as are we, to Death all hail

But no, I will not abandon the light

Nor dishonor her struggle, her selfless fight

For she is the flower that winter may now own

But when Spring arrives, she will rise again and be known

That is the part of the oath we must never forget

Never to give in to eternal sadness and regret

Strength comes from the dignity of those who are gone

As long as I recall the light that on me once shone upon

"Knowing your own darkness is the best method for dealing with the darknesses of other people."

C.G. Jung

INTUITION AT WORK

OCTOBER 2017

On the heels of a quite ordinary incident, I began thinking about how these pointless conflicts arise. Intuition, which is nothing more than preconscious perception, is mostly responsible, allowing things we notice but which don't get through th filer to consciousness. If we are aware of how this works, it can be an incredibly valuable source of insight. But if it escapes our awareness, things slip out putting a finger onto some raw nerve and provoking a violent response. Too often this can happen not just between individuals, but between nations with tragic consequences.

In the thirty years I was away

Living in a different world day by day

One doesn't see how things evolve

New assumptions, new challenges to solve

Shifts occur in how we see

Adapting to the ways of present reality

The past is shifted to the side

Making room, no need to hide

Eyes see facets, many new

Some resist, it's what others do

The former choose to ignore

The opportunity and what it's for

Simpler though not to change

An open mind can often derange

Years are spent to consolidate

The conflicting forces that operate

The glue can be of a different sort

The guardian of the ultimate court

For if a challenge questions its hold

One can answer present and be bold

But if the glue has hardened to its final stage

Each insult will provoke an irrational rage

The wagons circle, battle lines are drawn

The conflict won't wait for dawn

I have met this movement many times

Having spoken of them in rhymes

What was it I failed to see?

That lit the fuse, inevitably

A friend once mentioned, after a scene

When I stayed calm, and the other mean

Engage, she said, is what you do

Was this really something new?

We live a version of the present, thinking all is right

When the radar is on and we are ready to fight

All it takes is a word, innocent yet key

To set off the defenses always ready

No one came that day looking for a fight

Yet there it was, charging out of the night

A chip on the shoulder, some ancient wound unhealed-

*Lurking in the shadows, waiting to be revealed

It's there, we know it, so why the surprise?

Ignoring our own darkness is never wise

Why this sense of everpresent threat?

Your own demons, have you met?

For when we fail to look deep

Believing they have for good gone to sleep

They will raise their heads in surprise assault

Ambush, once engaged, one can rarely halt

Enmity is thus too often born

Before it's too late, we don't hear its horn

Insult, injury, poison flows

e watchful of these hovering crows

Ready to strike when least welcome

For them it's more like fun

Hold fast and ask them why

Do your best – at least try

"There is no coming to consciousness without pain"

C.G. Jung

TOTEM

December 2017

Those of you who have followed my work can't help but have been struck by the role all of Creation is "naturalize," i.e.returned to its true origins in the breadth of Nature. I do this as an antidote to the penchant we have to operationalize, anthropomorphize and there reduce the miracle of Life – all life. In more traditional cultures than ours, it was believed that animals represent our link to creation, often taking the shape of an animal. It is present in religious, myths, and even modern day mythology (e.g. Avatar).   This helped to avoid a sense of disonnectedness, of alienation from our world, explicit in the way in which we tend to ravage – beyond exploitation – nature. Cultures that had this link, even with their primitive scientific knowledged and often barbaric religious practices, did not feel the same sense of isolation we do. These animals represent something unique about us, bringing along their particularities – strength, wisdom, stealth, domination, etc.. And in times of true need, these peoples would turn to their special animal, their totem, for guidance and help when none is available from elsewhere. It is a psychic capacity to reach beyond the moment, the concrete, to realms where magic exists. I don't subscribe to the notion of true magic. But I do strongly believe that these totems are the source of our inner strength, capable of inciting us to rise to challenges we would otherwise consider beyond our reach.   It is a devastating observation to see this wondrous inner resource, this core of our resilience which removes feelings of isolation, and therefore powerlessness, disappear. Nature loses the protection we owe it. We lose the ability to transcend ourselves, particularly in times of great need. Everyone loses.

In times long past

In cultures that did not last

At birth each was given

As one's sins were forgiven

To start life fresh, with a special friend

One connecting us in a way that would never end

An animal, from Nature's realm

So when in need, to take the helm

To point the way to a place secure

This was a gift immense and pure

Now look what we have done

In the name of indulgent fun

These creatures, those who still roam wild

These beings that are Nature's child

Their magic lost to simple pleasure

All that's left of this immense treasure

Is to rescue us from our solitude

Ensuring a more stable mood

As our power has grown

As technology's seeds were sown

As what once ruled us all

As it now stands on the precipice, ready to fall

God like now, we seem to think

Our manufactured world could never sink

Yet signs appear from all points diverse

Things don't have to improve, they can also get worse

Now, when the temples built to our own glory

The end to a chapter takes shape to our story

Oh that these totems, the animals divine

Their friendship everlasting, their path a line

By their connection to this world we dismiss

Teach us once again the ground to kiss

For born of it, a part not apart

If only we could once again hear the beat of its heart

Reminding us all is not take

Before it's too late, that we awake.

FRIDAY

September 2017

This is one of the most difficult poems for me to have written for it goes back to an early childhood experience which marked me so deeply, that it set a course I never anticipated. It's a story of a love so pure only a child is capable of it. Of trust and how it was betrayed, not our of malice, but our of ignorance embraced. And how powerless a child can feel when confronted with the world of adults, with what they consider important decisions, whilst they are really only self-serving. There is no drama, only a sense that I could not defend that which could not defend itself. And to this day, I carry a regret so profound that I can never forget it. Loyalty – a word we use more in the negative, i.e. disloyalty,- to the point where its true beauty is close to being forgotten. Should that happen, I wonder if we could still consider ourselves as God's greatest creation, for other species seem far more capable of it than are we.

It was 1954, thought it was later

Hurricane Witch Hazel had struck, and it was a hater

My father, in one of our rare excursions

Took me to the seashore to observe the storms exertions

I remember the scene, even at that young age

For in my mind, associated events led to my first rage

Later in the week, as was our way

Chinese food once a week, and today it was Friday

I recall, after wonton and rice, and spare ribs having eaten

Walking to the car a boy approached with a black dog – weatherbeaten

He asked if we would give him a home

His mother forbid him, so he was alone

To care for this dog who'd been out in the storm

Though young he was sick and most likely forlorn

For years – though I was but 4 – I'd wanted a dog of my own

To be my best friend always, neither to ever again be alone

The next thing I knew we were in the car

On our way home, we lived not far

And next to me in the back seat

Was this dog who I loved at our first meet

I remember few things, and I cannot swear

The details are exact though the sentiment is there

He would sleep in my room, with me on the floor

For he was so big, of space he needed more

This was no sacrifice, what would I not do for this friend

And from his sickness, well did he mend

His strength returned and he started to grow

How big he would get, we did not know

But to me nothing mattered, for he was there

The world looked different to me – kind and fair

Friday, we named him for the day he was found

A big black dog full of love now on solid ground

The months passed, as our bond did grow

He was my friend, that's all I needed to know

My parents thought otherwise, for they had no clue

How to train or care for a dog beyond feeding and walking
– nothing else they knew

Of young dogs – or little boys – for that matter, neither
was truly understood

Friday had such energy, and would spend it to no good

Leap over the hedges to the neighbor's yard

Apologies flowed, apparently it was hard

But the coup de grace came when Friday chewed the couch

What's a couch, does it feel pain or love, to a boy? It's just a
grouch

A place not to play, no feet allowed

What is it, some sort of God, before which one bowed?

And so it was decided by others than me

That Friday must go, no discussion was there to be

Daddy would bring him to a place, a new home

He'd go "upstate to a farm" where he would be free to
fun and roam

Children, so trusting, believe such lies

Nonetheless, no one heeded my cries

For I was to lose my brother, my very best friend

What kind of a mess to a little boy is that to send?

I remember the scene, the Sunday morn

I was playing with my trains in the dining room, lost and
forlorn

My father returned having done the deed

Something deep in my soul was planted – a need

For in this life there are things that are wrong

One can try and smother their impact with words and song

But wounds such as this, proving first to me

How little what I thought or needed – none really cared
see

The lesson I learned on that day – though I spoke not to
my father or three whole days

Was just how disloyal people can be when a child's heart
one betrays

How utterly powerless I was made to feel

How was I ever from this wound to heal?

Children recover, at least so it may seem

I was of a forgiving nature, not inclined to be mean

But Friday marked my life in such profound ways

His memory will stay with e until the end of my days

For from that moment on, my values were set

Loyalty is forever or not at all – on that you can bet

And as I walk this earth in search perhaps of my dog lost

Though strong and capable, I pay the cost

Unable to abandon those in true need

For now and always, my heart will bleed

For I Friday I failed, it set the tone

Forever in my life that lapse will I atone

In those months we shared, I never felt alone

He was the first friend, and side by side we should have older grown

This is why when Lily was taken

My world once again was so shaken

Why I feel I failed a second time?

When He took a piece of my heart and thought that was fine.

From this place of pain and regret

There is no way or want to forget

Memories such as this are meant to endure

So that we never wound another with a wound that knows no cure.

Sadly, I have nothing but my memories and my regrets for Friday. So far as I can recall, this is something what he looked like. He deserved better.

A WORLD CHAOTIC, PARENTS ROBOTIC

December 2017

In a city such as New York, or any large city, for that matter, where we live on top of each other, it is hard not to assist at all kinds of interactions. Living near Central Park where parents and small children abound, I've noticed how much the nature of the relationship parent/child has changed. From the rigid formality of the past where parents were to be feared and respected, we have indulged our taste for the easygoing, The casual. Where once there was Father or Mother, there is now Bob and Carol. Where once authority came from Father, with Mother a second in command, we now have Nanny's manning the homefront while parents are out working to earn the money to pay the Nanny. There is a certain absurdity to all of this, as there is no greater task nor more important mission in life than, if one has chosen to have children, than to raise them. But I digress. Below are some thoughts derived from these observations. They are not meant to judge nor accuse. They are meant as food for thought. I hope it agrees with you.

The child's world is indeed chaotic

Parents assume their role at times in a manner robotic

Ill prepared in both example and disposition

Not yet having completed their own childhood transition

One might say it has always been so

How could such a task we come to know?

Memory fails. Recall our own example?

And was oneself from a representative sample?

Yet is there a task more important than this?

We often wonder if it was a hit or a miss

How to measure how much to give?

Though the expectation is to learn as we live

Perhaps here is a good place to start

Have we watched ourselves as we played our part?

Busy are we in so many ways

As they fly by, this rush of days

Two spouses working, who raises the child?

Whose task is it to be both firm and mild?

When so little time remains to nourish a mind

When disguised as freedom, can indulgence make us blind?

Think back now and ask, what sets you at peace?

Is it days filled with stuff, a moment of release?

Or rather is it that moment of silence

When danger recedes, leaving no scent of violence?

When someone else takes hold of the reins

So we can let go of the stress and the pains

Who is this wonder? Who can carry this weight?

For whom no task is too heavy, no burden too great

These are the moments when we realize

Just how much someone greater than ourselves we prize

If it was parents, lucky were we

If not, another it had to be

And in the absence of any substitute

The divine could work, none can refute

But in the end, who must that be?

The one who knows you best and will set you free

From dependence on others, whose priorities diverge

To influence each and every urge

To the one who will know, having learned

Themselves having been too often burned

Has this grown tiresome with my wordy evocations?

It's time now, you think, that I provide the key to relations

As if one key did exist

As if there was some secret list

A recipe, an answer that is ready made

To relieve us of the need to reflect, perhaps an expert that's paid

One whose study of children claims to have found the holy grail

So our children in all things a success will be, never to fail

But wait, success, what does that represent?

Must my child excel in every effort, is that what is meant?

I could continue, but fear your patience is wearing thin

Come on now, it's clear we all want to win

But win what? Is raising children a race?

What's more important in the end? The medals or the face?

Enough, I admit, so here we go

To really understand anything of value, it's essence to know

Time and effort, courage and care

That's the minimum required, along with fair

Conviction that comes from a deep and thoughtful place

And an authenticity – itself dearly bought – in every case

These are the things that a child does need

Parents, if you care, think on this, take heed

This task can't be delegated, no substitution allowed

If the commitment looks too great, if by it you are cowed

A child is a person, a life to be

If you are blind yourself, how can you child ever see

A Mother, A Father these are roles of great measure

And if you want the best for your precious little treasure

Then think not just of the joys and validation that may await

Think also of what it will take to get past each gate

Be strong, be firm, be clear, be most of all real

Teach them to win and to lose, and how to feel

No magic lies in the fact of two parents it was born

Each child will emerge different, as if from your fantasy torn

Repeat as often as you must for the message must be clear

You will be loved if committed, have no fear

Sense what transpires in yourself when conflict arises

Though conflict is something everyone despises

But most of all be sure, in this world uncertain

They know you will always be there, never dropping the curtain

For if they step onto the stage of life so

Sure of an honest backup, secure they will know

That if they fall down, as is required of us all

They will know to pick themselves up, and once again stand tall.

PART III

THEY WERE NEVER YOURS

December 2017

More words on the role of parents, though this time with a focus on the consequences for us all if certain needs are never met. Children are not little adults. They are beings in the process of becoming. Treating them as adults deprives them of the safety and security that only childhood can provide. If you'd want a friend, find one your own age. But if you have a child, be its parent. Some adults might even grow up themselves.

When a decision is made to have a child

When welcomed as a blessing, warm and mild

We imagine a little person, a future reflection

Endowed with all our dreams and predilection

One might say is has always been thus

So why now do we raise such a fuss?

The answer is simple and oh so clear

Our numbers and abilities are cause for fear

With little reason and less concern

We might set this planet alight to burn

Eliminating ourselves, which might not be all bad

Given how we wasted all the bounty we had

Returning now to child rearing, its rewards and trials

Should one not view the world as a child does, all heaps and piles

We assume it's natural to raise a child

After all, we were once ourselves young and wild

But who recalls what it was truly like?

After all, once learned, on never forgets how to ride a bike

Not so simple, though uncomfortable it may be

How can one understand another if their point of view we can't see?

I observe parents engaging children on matters of all kinds

With no thought at all as to what's in that creature's mind

Most seem to think if bound by some genetic link

They must see the world as we do, and therefore like us think

Nothing could be further from the truth if invented

A mind is owned for life, not for the short term rented

The world is a mass of swirling forces

Winds, rain, trees, wild horses

People both large and small

Noises, smells, how to make sense of it all?

First by perception – sight sound, smell and touch

Then by movement – for the physical world requires such

Interaction of all types and kinds

The world comes together in all of our minds

But since these components, though similar for most

Are also different from coast to coast

So convention demands education to complete the task

Some given by parents, some given by schools – one should always ask

Conflicts arise as versions differ ever more

Some principals we agree on, others we abhor

Add into the mix cultures varied and to us strange

Languages foreign further complicate exchange

In light of all this, let's now to parents return

Does anyone ever consider how much there is to learn?

But who is the teacher who has covered all bases?

Who can know what goes on behind these different faces?

So the task is reduced to a transactional state

Goals are set, piled high on the plate

The short term prevails, busyness rules

It seems we've concocted a recipe to raise several generations of fools

Can we survive, will the world outlast?

Our ignorant follies with these characters in the cast?

Excuses always ready at hand

Generic and loud, like some marching band

It's not good enough to do one's best

What will happen if we fail the test?

Is there anything more important than a soul can do?

Than be sure to transfer all that one knew

From the study of life, what experience has taught

More valuable than anything with money can be bought

A Parent is a function that should be written in capital letters

To ensure continuity beyond the trend setters

For the world of a child is fraught with fear

All is new and strange and at first, too near

How can a child view a parent always on the run?

Who speak less of caring and more of fun

Of their right to have it all, to somehow come first

How can the outcome be any but the worst?

When asking a child what it wants to do

Did you ever consider what the child really knew?

Of their options, and did they have the means to select

And why should a child an adult direct?

To place a child in a such a position

Can only spread doubt, confusion and indecision

Where a parent wants to let the child discover

Without the means to do so, one is removing the cover

Of security, of teaching, of the protection a parent provides

Is this not a better way than from inevitable conflict one hides

Benevolent authority. Clarity and explanation. Security and Stability.

These are the tools of any education of quality.

Fail and there can only be strife

For parents set the course of a life

Lives will be lost, the world is in play

There may indeed come once a final reckoning day?

LETTING GO

September 2017

More from the Chris Chronicles

I have had patients who, as my mentor once described, were "… the leftovers of God's anger." People who life had cheated so cruelly in different ways, one could only protest at the immorality of it. But since Life rarely listens to complaints of this sort. It is incumbent on us to right this wrong. In professional circles this is considered your typical counter-transference, where the psychologist projects onto the patient their own unconscious issues. I disagree, for we are first human beings, and only second whatever profession we exercise. When we see a wrong, there is a moral obligation to help. The problem is that too often the help we can provide is untimely or inadequate or both. But that doesn't change the necessity of showing one's humanity rather than hiding it behind some professional technique. For in the face of either the enormity of the wound or the untimeliness of the encounter, something positive should be lived at as deep a level as possible. Not all emotional baggage is bad. Some may return after having interrupted their own process, and I have found it impossible to deny them more often than perhaps was reasonable. But that Is just the point. Reason has little to do with these instances for these are the abandoned children of our world, starved of emotion. Any meal, if not a permanent solution, at least provides enough nourishment to continue. And the hope we can have for their salvation carries its own gifts to all concerned. It can help the fallen to rise again, bring a moment of peace to the persecuted, and a glimmer of light in a dark universe. And if that is the case, then perhaps there is a way out of hell after all.

Stories I hear, some I abhor

The path the impose, hard to ignore

How could this be to punish an innocent?

Taking a mind and making it bent

To set a child on a course that has no end

Where only pain will they know and no help to send

To abandon a young life with no love in their heart

It will matter little of their gifts, whether slow or smart

Against this injustice I feel a deep rage

Neutrality becomes just as impossible as turning the page

The reasons may be many and clear

The words may even be spoken without fear

But when one feels to the point of knowing

No more help can I give to keep them growing

Which leave me one last gift to give

That as they set off on their own, for as long as they live

To keep warm whatever was shared

Each in their own way, their hearts were bared

At this time perhaps it was not enough

Life can be cruel, heartless and tough

Yet in the face of such solitude

When all seems crass, angry and crude

To recall those moments of caring true

Even if they were the only ones they ever knew

How many times these words did I repeat

As if when reached out for I could ignore the heat

The burning pain deep inside

There is no place on this earth in which to hide

Yet when they return unexpectedly at my door

My resolve fades and I know what's in store

More of the same, though small progress is made

My friendship I cannot deny or have it forbade

To reenter our lives somehow believing anew

That during the hiatus, somehow they grew

Without acknowledging their progress, to send them away

And firmly instruct this can't continue this way

Would somehow betray the work that was done

And all the efforts paid sincerely that seemed to amount to none

I am a stubborn soul, slow to learn

For progress and caring I will always yearn

Not for me, for I no longer expect much from others

But for them, those I see cut adrift, be they sisters or brothers

No saint am I, for no holy mission is mine

I practice no ritual with blood or wine

But I live by that which I think is right

And if a wrong there is, and it deserves a fight

I will engage and do my best

To meet the challenge and pass the test

The years have given me opportunity to make this real

Commitment came easily, that how deeply I feel

And I have watched as those humbled managed to rise

No measurable miracle occurred that I could surmise

Others failed in their quest, for they never believed

And I have learned to accept this and am not aggrieved

But the hardest lesson, the one I struggle to learn

Is to know when the time has come to let the candle
just burn

Having done what I could, probably more than required

Others had seem how the light had expired

The conviction that only just one more try

And the light will shine through the darkest sky

I cling to this faith, though not much proof does exist

When I feel a call, it's hard to resist

But now I know it's more about me than whomever

No more pushing, the ties now I must sever

A part of me goes with them, I gave it in hope

But it was never meant to turn into a rope

Though we be made of base stuff, an inescapable fact

 Proven both in word, even more in act

So like Don Quixote, blinded o by his illusion

He saw what might exist, but in the end, it was delusion

So off you go, I do wish you well

Drop by if you want, new experiences to tell

But that kernel of a dream which I held for so long

That life to me never did belong.

Believe I will in the good that was done

If it wasn't enough, it was better than none

PROMISES I MADE TO MYSELF

July 2017

A rather cryptic exploration of the times when one is confronted with respecting the commitments one makes to oneself. It is for those situations when one's own weakness is engaged, fed often by a failure or a loss. For we find all sorts of crutches in our moments of need. But when the time comes to leave them behind, it's never that easy.

I've traveled too long on this wrong road

I've known it would lead nowhere, yet I persisted with my load

Until there was no mistaking, the signal came one day

For a time it had perhaps been the way

I trod this road in search of what had been lost

I'd grown weary of paying the cost

Fooled at first, believing what I did see

Wanting to believe this could a reality be

For some reason when down a path dark and wrong

I feel this truth, here I don't belong

The temptation is real, even if but for a short time

It seems all is good and I am once again fine

As I listened to myself explain again how an end must come to pass

Could I ignore this sign and would this day be the last?

Usually of an impulsive mind, now with a choice

As I've done so often before, I promised myself in a clear voice

Today I will close those doors, the one's I did not want sealed

And though there was some hesitation, my relationship was repealed

I knew it was the only way, old habits hang on tight

So easy to get comfortable while imagining one will win the fight

Hoping this change I would shuffle the cards well

Waking up to a new day freed, Life would surely tell

Speak to me of new opportunities and ways as yet unknown

Ready to meet this new day, new seeds waiting to be sown

At first seemed to appear a sign where I had abandoned hope

I thought there it is, the future is tending me a rope

My morning went by quickly, industrious as I could be

For I hoped that waiting was some new reality

What was expected did not arrive, and before I could react

An old surprise arrived unannounced, inviting me to act

Come have lunch with me, it will be my treat

This was unexpected, would I advance or retreat?

Only in books or stories are choices ever so clear

Decisions taken fearlessly may sooner than expected disappear

I thought but for a moment, emotions drove my choice

Nowhere, in this moment, was to be found the echoes of that voice

Lunch went well as my will returned to bring an end

This leads me nowhere, and no wounds would it mend

Nothing had changed that was tangible, or so it did seem

But something still felt right and I had not the heart to
be mean

Time was spent, words exchanged, suggestions of what
could be different

In the end, these resolutions were neither kept nor
meant

So the voice returned, chastising me again

A contract might help so I picked up paper and a pen

The next day, again unexpectedly, a surprise appeared

This time anger held, no indulgence was to be feared

More efforts to reach out arrived, each one ignored

Certain this time, no further chances had been stored

Persistence can mean two things, one good and one bad

Good means it's on the right path, bad just means sad

So when, in the face of cold rejection met

Another wager was made, another bet, and yet

Explanations offered, unsure if false or true

Something subtle did seem different, a possibility new

In the end what to think? Was I smart or just being dumb?

Should I allow this seed that refuses to die and let myself go numb?

Reason best shines its light on situations black or white

The heart, though it can be thus, at times requires an extended fight

To confront those forces pulling in opposite directions

To burn away impurities and purify affections

Perhaps in the end, the result will be the same

For in matters of the heart, one must play out the game

Where what's at stake is simple, a diversion at best

But if a life is on the line, one must pass the test

A heroic view of life perhaps, filled more with pain than hope

But if one see's another drowning, can one really pull the rope?

Is that the promise I spoke about at the beginning of this rhyme?

No I idea it would take this turn, believing I'd drawn the line

 Watch this space for future news from the same byline

Reason tells me one of two things, neither of which looks that fine

Either this will be but yet another repetition

Or small steps going forward may end in a positive rendition.

Ignoring what the future holds, isn't that always the case

Patience will be required, but cannot set the pace

I will hold fast until my heart is convinced

If this thing will remain or be evinced.

REVERSING POLARITY

August 2017

*This poem is perhaps a good example of how poetry can slip through the normal rational filters by refusing to obey the laws of narrative and temporality. There are so many metaphors, I can't point them all out. But, for example, every image evoked suggests a danger, something that might come apart, though there is no **explanation or sequence**. Then there is the matter of the narrative (indosofar asthere is one), which has some semblance of order, but not enough to make it clear. To follow this poem, one cannot rely on the roles of prose where the plot line is constant. Just these few issues are sufficient to confuse a reader who comes with expectations which have nothing to do with the message. One knows it is there, but it's just not obvious. So, one has two choices: first, to complete the work, as if nothing ever happened. .Or, the other is to open one's mind to the transmission, and set aside the normal logical structure of language, and like water, let it seep in, believing that once assimilated, it will make sense. And to my surprise and great pleasure, and though it hasn't changed anyone's life, people appear to be a bit more engaged because more aware of what is really going on. Poetry can relax by its rythms, soothe by its music, release the mind through the language of metaphor, and if everyone is lucky, something which would otherwise have been rejected, somehow made it in. Isn't that the point?*

There are always 2 sides to everything

One shines like some light reflecting

The positive side, full of hope

 Pointing a way to grow and cope

And then there is the dark side

Its purpose less clear when it chooses to hide

The mysterious secrets, not easily revealed

Like some cryptic message in an envelope sealed

To decode the ciphers takes effort and time

For they are nuanced, that undersanding must refine

In these words their purpose lies hidden

Find the key and possess the treasure forbidden

For the dark truth, most powerful than all

Unlocks the beast until then, held in thrall

Knowing, yet untamed

Recognized, still unnamed

Bringing the two together, a task of great skill

A savvy blend of patience, courage and will

Not to be blown away once the power released

Or be consumed all at once, as if at some feast

Transforming a life, until then flat and of little savor

Into a lifelong meal, full of new things and flavor

For those who see what most choose to ignore

Face a blank wall and an imposing door

Held in stasis, alive though not living

The days pass by, always the same unforgiving

To watch vitality spent for no gain

Often accompanied by boredom's pain

Options, clearly lying ahead

Met with a regard, blank and dead

And when appears a new perspective

A chance to move on and finally live

The atmosphere changes, negativity and doubt

One can watch, as hope gives out

Some have made this hole into their mount

Each step backward they'd rather count

Reversing polarity, defining by the naught

Such waste, early on they must have been taught

But like in some arachnid's web caught

Only against hope have they ever fought

Strange how the world can stand on its head

When optimism is replaced with dread

When the only purpose in one's life that can be found

Is to take one's potential and run it into the ground

To make of life the enemy

Blaming creation and refusing to see

The fault flows from choices we make

Empty inside, we know only to take

For if life feeds on itself, ironically

Like a fire, the more it is fed, it should burn more brightly

Never consumed by its own flames

Direct, never playing foolish games

Raging with energy, like the sun

Existing to warm all things and each one

Get too close, and one will burn

Stay too far, and never learn

So simple, yet for some so out of reach

It's observation, not some theology to preach

So open your eyes if you dare

Live your life, if you can still care.

The wounds of the past unknown it is how to restore

Yet the holes they drilled go to straight to the core

To hear a silent call, and feel the pain

Is empathy designed only for gain?

A bond takes shape, there is a pull

One begins to wonder if a heart can be full

One that yearns but to give

And a mind that needs to be engaged to live

If all you know is how to take

You are for sure not yet awake.

We are given a life, to live but one

Is its purpose only wealth and fun?

Defend it you must, so get a gun

That's not living – it's life on the run

Hold fast to whatever you possess

Children run amuck, finances a mess

The wife has left, unless like you she too is lost

She buys what she wants but ignores the true cost

Nothing responds to rhyme or reason

Chaos is your only season

Hold on for as long as you can

If this was the only way you plan

Look around you – is there still a fan?

See who you've become – a lonely man

On the outside all looks well

Thank God the packaging won't tell

Fit as a fiddle with an exceptional tan

Make believe for as long as you can

In the end, centripetal forces at play

Have wreaked havoc on how we live each day

Science tells us the poles someday might invert

And stand us all on out head so we need be alert

Yet long before the cataclysm is here

There is a danger that is far more near

The order in line with who we are

Is being tugged on from afar

The things we thought were as supposed to be

Traditional values we thought could outlast eternity

Not so it seems, the gluejas lost its ability

When the world stands on its head, reversing polarity.

STARTING SMALL

August 2017

Having worked in a few large multinational corporations, I was always amazed at how well they seemed to work. That is, until I saw my first serious recall. In the grand scheme of things, it was a recall – the product had become inadvertently contaminated. The risk of any serious consequences was small, and indeed, everything was fine. Contrary to popular belief, this was a company in a category much vilified. Nevertheless, they went back to the beginning of the entire preparation process, cleaned every machine, brought back every piece that might carry the contamination, the packaging, and even the trucks. The cost was in excess of $250 million for an innocent accident. Or consider the Volkswagen emissions scandal which cost them in the billions – not that money is the best measure. Here is the States we do this systematically, rushing to get things out the door to start bringing in revenue, confident that should something go wrong, we can spin our way out of it and fix it later. But when they fail, and we often ignore the cost because it is rarely reported as such, the guilty parties have often moved on. I knew some attorneys at a Midwest, quite prominent law firm. Truly the salt of the Earth. They had an 11th Commandment. Don't get caught.   If this is the way things happen, if we no *longer see any reason to acknowledge mistakes, how can we ever learn?*

In these times of deep division

When the favored currency is derision

When trust is a must

Yet turns out to be a bust

When everyone talks

Yet at hearing, balks

When questions go unaddressed

Though they are posed at our behest

Whether they be for business or in our personal lives

If it's for the answer that one truly strives

The place to start is at the beginning

To have any chance of ever winning

For there are few questions that have never been asked before

Smarter people possibly made their own way to the door

Mistakes were made, errors found

Within what came before great treasures can still be found

But in our rush to convert solutions to money

Time was reduced in scope, and that's never funny

Cut here, cut there, we'll figure it out later if it fails

Thus began some of the greatest modern fairy tales

For in our lives racing from here to there

With a check list prepared with the utmost care

I never realized how great it could feel

To tick off each item – so organized, so real

Yet I can predict with unfailing certainty

You will forget something – wallet or key

For no one seems to recall

By which door they entered the hall

But choose at random where to begin

Unaware of the size or origin of the sin

For every answer to any question worthwhile

One must begin at the bottom of the pile

To detect, as with every tree

It all starts – though invisible – by the root, you see

How simple the thought to begin at the start

And follow its path through every part

Checking to see if sense is made

Each element connected as required, errors forbade

This life flows easily, no blockage or knot

Why then do we start in a middle spot?

Do we just assume that whatever came before

Since "old," one needn't consider it anymore

To do so would cost time and money

So let's just decide not to worry. You cool with that honey?

Let's plunge right in, we've got a process that works

Those consultants showed us, and they are no jerks

We payed them a ton, and they wowed us with smarts

Do you think they might also be good at playing darts?

Anyway, we plug this in here, and plug that in there

Once the data starts streaming we've nary a care

For the black box – it's the secret sauce

Doesn't tell us in detail what's happening inside – they are the boss

And out it comes, the answer statistically sure

All we need do is do what it says, voila – the cure

So the big day arrives, presentation in hand

The only thing missing are the fireworks and the band

We begin to explain what we ourselves ignore

Let's hope there are no questions – God what a bore

But If there are, and the answers we cannot provide

We'll just have to throw up some fairy dust and run and hide

Phase I of Recovery – ask for more time

Phase II of Recovery – say the fault isn't mine

Phase III of Recovery – have someone to blame

Phase IV of Recovery – be ready, if possible, with a name

Phase V of Recovery – say you will draw up a plan

Phase VI of Recovery – don't forget the budget for an extra man

Phase VII of Recovery – Milestones, of course, to track our progress

Phase VIII of Recovery – Schedule the first meeting for Project Redress

Phase IX of Recovery – Promise it will be right this time

Phase X of Recovery – Convince yourself the outcome will be just fine

Some levity to hide some tragic mistake

Pies we may make, but do we recall how to bake?

Look back to errors made in the pas

Consider the cost benefit of starting off too fast

Recall what happens when steps are skippe

And how it hurt falling down those steps on which we tripped

Plodding along, making sure it will work

Do we really want to storm off half cocked like some band of Young Turks

Each solution requires many things

Unless we've only geniuses, princes and kings

To solve any problem, however, one must think

A mental cramp has seized control, and broken the vital link

When did corruption capture our souls?

When did lying cease taking its tolls?

When did the we became me?

And when did I lose the ability clearly to see?

For what really counts, since numbers rule

s to have the most powerful numerical tool

For if there are no numbers – a language not everyone speaks

The damn will surely spring several leaks

Then the dance truly begins

As attempts to cover up seeks to bend the rules

How many times have we seen in the past

The crime may be small, but the cover up will always last

In all things which break, requiring a fix

We have two approaches to put in the mix

The first is to jump believing all can be repaired

After all, in the past we've often so dared

But thinking back, one conclusion is clear

Aside from not doing the crime, of the cover don't go near

Some things can't be fixed, how can we know

I we back to the beginning fail to go

THE CONUNDRUM OF CHANGE

October 2017

Jung spoke of an archetype her referred to as the Persona, or the mask, the interface we constitute with reality. It starts to emerge with the first corrections we experience, refining progressively our public face. It is obviously useful, for some more than others, since without it, here would be little chance for conformity, consensus, society, perhaps even civilization. But what happens when the link between ourselves and the Persona starts to fray, simply because we come to identify with the Persona, forgetting all the rest. It is our exterior, the wrapping, but not the substance. One cannot live without substance, for nothing then matters. It is an empty place, full of fear and anxiety because certitude resides with the outside, over which we have no control, and which follows its own rules. All we can do is follow. Look around you, think of your acquaintances and friends. See if you see the mask. If you look, you will. And you might even recognize your own.

There are periods in life when change is required

New challenges unsuccessfully unaddressed in stagnation mired

When one can no longer invoke the old solution

Toxic concentrations build with no benefit from dilution

They start to shrink, frustration abounds

No wise words arrive, only annoying sounds

A crossroads is reached in a case such as this

We find a way to go forward, or if a turnoff we miss

Backwards we go, deeper into the past

Those things left behind have managed to last

Our regard is drawn back to whence we came

The rules are all different in this new game

These are moments when fate intervenes

Help arrives at times in the shape of dreams

To provide a regard from the other side

The one from which we always sought to hide

But a dream is a point of view, not a solution

Not always does life favor an individual's evolution

So here we are, looking into the unknown

Where we came from we know, how the seeds were sown

Much pruning occurred, harsh winds have blown

In spite of it all, older we've grown

It all came together in the form of a mask

It became who we are and set us a task

To conform to its lines, hewing close to form

After all, we're expected to resemble some variant of the norm

And this is the problem that over the years takes shape

For the lines are written also by others, words from which we can't escape

If such is the case, if all we do is repeat

There is to be nothing new to be said as we face defeat

Some find the means for the mask to release

A space is created where fresh air does not cease

To nourish what was buried behind

Thus come into being new words to find

All is not over, the battle not done

For the mask remains, the war not won

Before there was one, an identity forged

With illusions and untruths its whole life was it gorged

Having taken on an existence of its own

Not so willing to cede its place, its home

-

And so begins the battle for change

Two forces opposed, much to derange

The mask is familiar and has become oneself

Whatever is possessed in reality, whatever one's wealth

Is owed to the mask, for it is the one

Who dealt with the world, who fought, lost and won

Providing what looked like a purpose, a direction clear

Ensuring security, holding at bay one's fear

To say goodbye to he who provides

On whose wings through life one glides

It may not be perfect, is familiar good enough?

What am I really made of, do I have the right stuff?

This new thing that promises renewal and more

It's a stranger to me, is it lover or whore?

It says it comes from a higher place

To shine a new light on a brand new face

To open a door that before wasn't there

An answer, a new hope, without a care?

But wait, I hear voices coming from within

I know who they are, they're not ready to give in

A dangerous wager trading familiar for the unknown

Will the earth be fertile to the new seeds sown?

This is the moment when we will know

The choice is made to exist or grow

No wager comes safely, much must be risked

At the border our mask we surrender to the guards as we
are frisked

Do we cross over? There is a cost

To change means to give up what we had – but must all be
lost?

To make way for whatever the future may hold

The road of life is filled with the bodies of so many bold

But such is Life, if one is searching for gold

One can also find oneself left out in the cold

Yet the eternal question remains unanswered still

Is it better to try, believing in the thrill

Or hold fast to safety, content to remain

Where one was born, never changing, like a stain

Live without risk is not life at all

Wise or foolish, at some time we all hear the call

Why do some respond, while others remain mute?

To follow the Pied Piper and his flute

Numb to everything that might challenge their plac

Preferring to remain on the sidelines rather than enter the race

Judgemental? Perhaps implicitly so

But that's what I've lived, so it's all I know.

THE DARK KNIGHT

August 2017

A metaphorical musing of one way of looking at the unconscious, this thing which we implicitly have decided not to consider very much since it cannot be empirically studied. I find this amusing as it is more a reflection of our insistence on imposing rational requirements where they logically do not apply. Can anyone deny that an "unconscious" exists, but since we can touch it, talk to it, dissect it, operationalize it to any empirical requirement, we simply dismiss it as a place to put all phenomenon we can't explain. It's the third eye we have, but which we cover up. Here I describe it as the place where, under pressure from our environment – mostly human – parts of ourselves are rejected whole in accordance with societal norms. In and of itself, this isn't a bad thing. But one should never throw the baby out with the bathwater. Why? Because this isn't bath water. These things we excise are part of a whole, and every organism is richer when all of its parts are mobilized. Fortunately, we are made in a way to seek balance, whence comes the Dark Knight. Out of the unconscious he emerges bringing stories,

At the dawn of our lives when all waits to be learned

Each day brought new discoveries, some welcomed, some spurned

Our vision of life being molded each day

Do you know who guided you and told you what to say?

It sounds so gentle when written on this page

Thinking back, can you feel a tingle of rage?

For though unformed and as yet undefined

Those surrounding us chisel away of our emerging mind

Thinking they are helping to ensure the best

Rarely if ever, their views are truly put to the test

Each has a vision of itself, updated by each

And expressed with conviction in thought and speech

Mother sees father in a certain way

A view she will repeat each and every day

There may be facets for each circumstance

But the song and music guarantee it's the same old dance

And Father, a participant in more mind, less heart

Sees Mother more function, less a partner, as it grows
 from the start

Sister, she of complex, conflicting emotions

More a construct than a person, floating on violent oceans

Barely tamed, yet born of fire

Never a truthteller, always a liar

And little brother, a son, often desired

More by mother than he by whom he was sired

The trinity thus violated, the turbulent peace was broken

Rarely if ever was the truth really spoken

Father would work, eat, sleep and provide

Never revealing himself, from the world to hide

Though on the surface, a smile for all

One could have thought he saw life as a ball

And so it went, this odd mix of souls

Why alone was he the one wanting to make himself whole

For the others bathed in the world this familiar brew

Was it that before he arrived, they'd already formed a crew

A set of shared values, unspoken but strong

To which they unknowingly subscribed so they could belong

Did they ever examine things or seek a perspective new?

Some people can swallow, others need to chew

Now if you are a reader, thoughtful and keen

And though the tone of this writing is neither angry nor mean

You may have noticed I too did what I earlier decried

See how easy it is to onself be lied?

I presented an image albeit brief yet clear

And no one objected, at least I didn't hear

Claiming no fault, for it's a practice tried and true

This is how our image of ourselves is created and brought into view

This would not be so grave if it were there to end

Each would go off on their journeys, these roles to test and to mend

But such is rarely the case, the bonds of family are strong

And the tethers that attach us can last a life long

Like a sculpture that started out full and round

With each comment, a flaw to be excised is found

Assisted self-multilation, how's that for an idea?

For the scalpel employed is ridicule and fear

And there being no bin for the bio-waste

No bandages are provided, it's done in haste

Disposed of in an inaccessible place

To live forever like some dark race

These innocent prisoners who've done no wrong

Dark forces they send in sleep, to them does the night belong

Images, some familiar, others strange

Contexts unearthly at times our sleep to derange

Violent or peaceful, from paradise to hell

Why do they come and what do they tell

Now think for a moment, what is this dark place

Where in our mind does it hide, leaving no solid trace

But these images, furtive, fleeing the day

And what is their language trying to say

They come from us, from all that we have perceived

Too much comes in so to be relieved

A sorting occurs, some remain present in our mind

The rest is archived in a place none can find

But it can find us, should we wander too far afield

From the center, some answers to yield

How can that be, they seem to make no sense

Oh but they, for they live in no fixed tense

Time there obeys no clock

It's infinite spaces knows no lock

Stories it tells, through evocation

Taking our minds on a necessary vacation

To see things we otherwise block

When we need to pause and truly take stock

Not in some self-interested way

Seeking validation to get through the day

To look to the past, present and future as if one

So complete its vision, no need to jump the gun

From this place may ride a savior not yet recognized

He carries messages that should be prized

The tell us of ourselves, of parts we ignore

To show us how our wholeness to restore

Is that the silver bullet, the answer to it all

Or is it a joining together, a clarion call

For he is the Dark Knight, there when we need

If only we take note, and his words we heed

THE LAST STRAW

From The Chris Chronicles

November 2017

Possibly the last entry in what I have called the Chris Chronicles, for I sensed something had broken, something so reminiscent for him of the depth of pain he felt when a child, something he never wanted to experience with me, but knew he would eventually provoke it. He said two things the last time I saw him. The first was "…I don't want to die alone," and as he ran away, I hear a child's complaint "…don't yell at me like that." I knew he wasn't really talking to me, but to his mother, and every other adult who treated him as unwanted and a nuisance. It was a very sad moment, and when I raised my voice to him – as he had done with me and I had done with him many times before – this time it was different. It wasn't my last straw. I fear it was his. He wasn't angry with me. He was angry with himself for having brought down my anger on him for nothing of any great importance, as he had done a thousand him to the core.

The struggle has lasted more than 3 years

I have watched him face and give in to his fears

His fantasies approaching mental disease

Have a root in reality, but appease

The story that's sad

Turned a good boy bad

But a choice was given, a hand extended

Yet each time, the truth was upended

For his true connection was to a drug

And with its help, his hole he dug

So often offered a choice that was clear

And for a short time, a struggle seemed to appear

But in the end, each and every time

He chose no reward, only the fine

On the run, looking over his shoulde

All that awaits is him getting older

And if this flight to nowhere good

That takes him back to his old hood

Can only end in one place

A blanked out mind and an emptied face

I have tried my best

Certainly more than the rest

But when something so fundamental as to connect

Is lacking, one can only dissect

To discover at the root

Was a hole. a blank space – the rest is moot

Those like him can mimic what's real

But in the end, they never learned to feel

Survival is all life has taught

And in societies net he will someday be caught

And won't manage to wiggle his way free

Once in the clutches of psychiatry

Medicated to the max, pushing a broom

Institutionalized, sharing a room

And all that potential will wither away

And he will push the same broom every day

Disappointed? For sure, for I will always believe

And hope that change can come to relieve

For every story is self-explanatory

And should make it easier to find some glory

In mobilizing the heroism to face down one's fears

And wash one's soul clean, with all those tears

That were never shed, but swallowed, extinguishing life's fire

So run, Chris, run, and never tire.

Why do I do this, pick the wrong soul?

Am I not clear to myself, and am close to whole

Do I need to find another so badly incomplete

Equivalent in darkness, and with light I am replete

Do I seek the miracle I managed on myself

Effecting in another a great source of emotional wealth

But the odds are small, success rare

How can it happen in a world that doesn't care?

But to feel is to live, and to live is to share

Not hide behind an illusion, safe from any dare

THE MASK

November 2017

Too often struck, as we all have, by the inadequacy of facsimile, I took some time, perhaps too much, to reflect on what it means to abandon the search for who we are in favor of slipping on a socially acceptable mask, often handed down. Over time, one simply loses track of who one is, focused more on recasting the mask to suit the current preferences or demands. Just think of what happened to Michael Jackson. He got lost inside himself, and not finding a way home, thought by changing his mask to reflect what he thought was desirable, he could find himself. How could that ever work?

This thing we wear all day long

Perfected over time, so we can belong

Resembling to the point of acceptance

So we can enter into life's dance

Social Creatures, we are born this way

To fit in we struggle every day

Fine tuning so as to please

For very few does it come with ease

The music written, not by us

Can I sit out the dance? Would that raise a fuss?

To differentiate is to stand apart

Is it allowed to write one's own part?

Great of small, known or not

The first task - to discern the prevailing plot

The role to play, actors all

In unison please, so as not to fall

When did life become so?

Who writes the lines that we must know?

That when our turn finally arrives

The words are spoken to reflect our own lives

Forgetting that behind the mask

Was one who forgot the essential task

The one we are given when we are born

The one that too quickly can prick like a thorn

At odds with how others wish to see

Once it begins, are we ever again free?

Ready to be remolded as needed

Stripped of its soul, it goes unheeded

To grow thus, always honing one's mask

To the point where what's behind it no one will ask

Having never shown its one true face

How could others see if never shown a trace?

That is the day when one's sees one's fate

Its end is in sight, no need to wait

Unless, of course, the unexpected changes the game

When the mask no longer works who's to blame?

Confusion ensues, what to do?

Take a look inside and find out who

Was living unknown, hidden, alone

Was a sin ever committed for which to atone?

Remove the mask, let the day shine in

Imagine for once, this is how you can win

Feel the air on your face, the sun as well

Realize that where you were living was a personal hell

All the struggle to please those who don't care

To yourself, be honest, but also be fair

Why else to be here but to know?

Incomplete we are but well equipped to grow

Into what you ask? What is the goal?

What does it mean to become more whole?

Will it bring me fortune, love or fame?

If there no money in, why be in that game?

If the greatest privilege in this life

Is not to accumulate great wealth or only avoid all strife

Or to marry a beautiful trophy wife

Or that ridiculous set – the Ginzu Knife

The answer may seem small – it's insight

To see pick a one true side and stop the fight

To look at the world with a clarity that's new

More certain for once of what's real and what's true

Armed thusly provides no magic solution

Life is often chaotic, often ablaze with revolution

But with all parts of oneself working in synch

No longer is it necessary the KoolAid to drink

Authentic. Sincere. Real. Caring

These are the tools a full life should bring – daring!

So that when looking back on the path that was taken

One's faith in oneself have become consolidated, not
shaken

 A coming together, each piece finding its place

 A mosaic of great beauty, visible on your face

Time slows down as less remains

A blending made of joys and pains

But keep the pieces apart, locked hidden in place

Avoiding recognition wearing a mask not a face

How can something made of disparate parts

Ever succeed to win any hearts?

> *"Masses are always breeding grounds for psychic epidemics"*
>
> C.G. Jung

IT CAN HAPPEN HERE

December 2017

Having grown up in New York City where there was little blatant anti-semitism, so when I went to live in Switzerland, supposed land of refuge for the Jews during the Second World War, I expected none. Though superficially, everything went smoothly, there were a few instances, even with my Swiss in-laws. It wasn't intentional. It was reflexive. When Mario Cuomo began his crusade against the Swiss banks for their dealing with deposits made by fearful Jews in the 1930s, I saw something I did notexpect. The wagons circled, rational people espoused nonsensical rumors supposed to explain why these noble Swiss were being so falsely accused. I won't go into the details of my experience, for they are personal and anecdotal. But the impact they had on me was to make me realize that what happened in Europe in the 1930s and 1940s was not by accident. And I realized that rational people are capable of irrational, hateful actions when two conditions are met: they feel threatened in some fundamental way, and when – and this is rarely a coincidence – an individual arrives with a negative, hateful, divisive message which, through its voice, can galvanize disparate innocuous groups into a national force capable of great evil. Moderates tend to dismiss this as of little concern or readily managed by establishment forces. And by then, it might just be too late. Look closely, listen carefully, at what is going on here. Ring any bells? Yes. It could happen here. A cautionary tale of what happens when strains appear and how, if not vigilant, what once defined gets turned inside out. When we stop considering accountability, when we take our values for granted, when we find it easier to blame those weaker than ourselves, when we find our civic responsibilities too intrusive, and when we are witness to a wrong, we say nothing......that's when the dark forces have arrived and it may already be too late.

Who amongst us recognizes the signs?

When a negative affect crosses infects our lines

From the neutral zone where balance can prevail

And we all like to think its from here we hail

Its form can resemble an explosion that can shake the walls

Unleashing with a vengeance a rage from within that calls

For it all to tumble in the face of such force

Splitting asunder what was once was, a frightful divorce

Departing as quickly as it arrived

And begin we can to see what has survived

The rubble is cleared, edifices again rise

As if it never happened, a vale of lies

Trapped, the author of the conflagration

Giving rise to the birth of a new nation

Or

t can take a form more subtle, which most ignore

Slowly but surely, a darkness descends, no one knows what's in store

The anger can be cold as surely as hot

Together in a cauldron they churn full of ooze and rot

Where the evil therein, heated by the fire

Imagining a purification where it can expire

But the flames, quite the contrary, favoring a transformation

For from this dark soup will arise a dark new nation

Built on the very thing that defines its soul

Anger and resentment will have made it whole

Given a face, a voice, a message and direction

If it flows not from our declared predilection

Old truths are deformed, undetected by reason

How easy it becomes, this national treason

The music plays, they dance along

To that which gave them birth, they no longer belong

Goodbye to who they were, thinking there to return

The past goes up in smoke, their soul they burn

Looking back to the past instead of ahead

When heart and mind are no longer properly fed

One can grow hot, all passion and haste

The other grow-s cold, for revenge,develop a taste

Define then separate, identifying first the weak

A curse on our unit, of this speak

Eliminate this drain on what makes us great

Love is gone, replaced by hate

The institutions which watch over us well

 We can recall perhaps of a time before they fell

With none to protect us, fear reigns

For a time it might work, immediate easy gains

Those who are different are no longer here

Yet we continue to bicker, driven by fear

For hate is a fire that burns so cold

Consuming everything, young or old

Once the other has been dealt with, it craves something new

Turning on itself, there's nothing else to do

That's how it happens, a child of fear

And just remember, it could – if we let it – even happen here

The unimaginable can happen, now you see

Why we all must speak up in the name of unity

Those who pour venom on those unalike

In their path they leave cracks in the dike

One simply truth, one fact above all

Together we rise. Apart we will fall

TIME AND ITS THREE CHILDREN

NOVEMBER 2017

A reflection on Time, and it's three children – past, present and future. It seems the first two have grown while the third has shrunk. When did the future, built on progress, become an object of fear? At a time when we live perhaps better than any of our predecessors, we seem to believe the contrary. Have we grown soft, lazy and self-indulgent, costing us the courage and the hope that alone can carry us to a better place? I leave it to you to decide.

Often referred to as Father Time

He was seen as slow moving and benign

Immutable to the point only the old took note

His sole job moving forward and never gloat

But in the background other forces were at work

Three they in his shadow did they lurk

First came the Past, unmistakable and real

Who could deny his existence for all did feel?

His passage marked by the stones on which lives are built

Providing two faces, one of pride, the other guilt

The balance of the two defines each life

Made of unequal parts of joy and strife

Next comes the Present, the one spoken most about

Linked to sensations, drives and hungers, it carries the most clout

In a constant succession of moments flowing into each other

Its existence over once it began , a fugitive brother

But what we forget, living in the present alone

We forgive the immediate past, and with it the need to atone

Transgressions committed dissolve as if they never were

Engendering a current favorite, denial, born of the blur

And what of the third child, who might that be?

The Future, of course, how could we not see?

A pregnant question. Is the answer still born?

Too many Presents from the fabric of time are shorn

If the now alone counts, the future ceases to exist

And with it the faculties we were given – they cease and desist

Abstract thinking, to create what was never before seen

A diminished creation, we begin to grasp and grow mean

In times of plenty, generosity comes with ease

When things start to lack, greed appears like a disease

The future is built on a foundation defined the Past

Most solid of all and meant to last

The Past with its legacy of the good and the bad

A mix of emotions, from happy to sad

No one emerges from the lost before

Without a need to correct what need be in store

Yet not immune to growth and change

Progress can come if we fear not to derange

Embrace a faith in a better place that can be built

A future born of courage and hope, we now can at windmills tilt

If this makes no sense to most, though they define who we are

And with them are set high or low our values ,and the bar

Our vision myopic, we cease to look far

Disaster awaits when a sightless driver holds the wheel of the car

Two without three of Time's children, a family incomplete

We turn on ourselves, and dial up the heat

The road to the future frees us alone the way if we so choose

Look up at the limitless sky, for if not, ourselves we will surely lose.

THE SMILING TOAD

OCTOBER 2017

A rather dark musing on choices one makes, on a day when the usual answers to troubling questions failed me. Whether or not there is any wisdom here, it is always best to take a serious look by committing, critically, open-mindedly, honestly, to paper what is really going on. It may seem whiney. It may even be whiney and self-serving. But with practice and a keen eye, one learns to be a better, and helpful, friend to oneself.

I've always done things my own way

Not that I'm a rebel, always seeking to stray

Or undermine the prevailing style

In fact, I often fit in with a smile

But one thing seems to always block my road

I'm not sure where hides this evil toad

For though I fear not to take the lead

And see something better, and not from greed

I want to have them come to me

To bring them into my world so they can see

To feel its completeness, its certitude

This is not some empty attitude

The one, the center, that which guides my way

Lies inside me, for I feel it every day

Others feel its pull and are drawn to my side

At first there is openness, no desire to hide

But then a change starts to take shape

Cracks appear for which there is no tape

Up to the line that they must cross

To leave the past and become the boss

Not of anything, but of their own lives

There is no need for violence, nor guns, nor knives

And so at this place of fateful decision

Occurs now an expected division

Why, I wonder, is this again the end?

Does their North Star another destination send?

Were they seduced by something they saw in me?

Thinking the solution lied simply in proximity

Or is there an answer more simple to find?

No one can cross the line with a borrowed mind

So often this happens, are we so few, lonely is the star's direction

That many will cross my path without election

So far, none has been fated to hold my hand

If ever I am to reach that promised land

A promised, the ultimate illusion?

Who spoke such words of fateful delusion?

The journey by laught has been wrought

And our kind has so many battles fought

There is no hand there, guiding the way

As Life presents itself every day

Coherence comes from how we choose to live

Some seek answers and try to give

To share what little they have learned

Odd how so often wisdom is spurned

For free is too low a price to pay

If anything is to be ours and can't be taken away

Is this gift I've spent my life to build?

Better than most I've found more empty than filled

What is it worth and to who?

It seems a question of degree, but few

We live our lives in a collective state

Which determines so much of our fate

But that part, the one which remains

Can change the state of losses and gains

Some seize the tillar so they can choose

Hoping to win more often than lose

There is a cost to this prideful choice

One came to speak a foreign voice

The words may sound just the same

But their meanings mark the changing game

With each passing year the distance grows

The more one becomes oneself, the more one knows

The less the others understand

As it starts to feel like a foreign land

The question then is was it worth the cost?

I may have found myself, but the other was lost

Others may leave it up to fate

Accepting whatever fall into their plate

Questions for them occupy little space

They run in tandem as they race

To a destination they ignore

As they pile through the open door

But in this crowd, they stand not alone

All they do is whatever is known

And what is the price they must pay?

Alone inside, each and every day

A third way, perhaps, the most confounding of all

Is somewhere in between where they stall

Half measures won't often prevail

Should one not seek shelter when it starts to hail?

Or will it soon stop and be done?

Mistakes, however necessary, are never fun

Indecisive, confused, anxious, abused

At the very best, life defused

So there you have it, as close as I've come

Have I started at last more clearly to some?

Do I like what I have now revealed

Will it comfort my soul and see me healed?

Or is it just the end of the road?

And sitting there, a smiling toad

IN NEED OF NEW DIRECTIONS

September 2017

If you've ever felt stuck, when old solutions failed you, read on. When you feel the need to move forward, but just don't know how? If life has stalled on you, it's always a good idea to ask yourself this.question: What might Life be telling me that I am not getting? Has it all changed and I didn't see it happening? Out of synch, out of step, somehow not seeing what I knew was there.....

Is it really possible that life can stall?

That everything stops in front of a wall

When all your life you've stood tall

Not afraid to take risks and maybe fall

Close enough now to have what you want, if not all

Why now has Life chosen to stop and stall?

For in this time when a corner is turned

And every initiative appears to be spurned

I wonder at times what keeps me going

Though to where that is I have no way of knowing

What other option exists that might await?

Is it there? I just can't seem to find the gate

For my path has been different, I have no regret

All in all, I've not done badly in placing my bet

But why then when I am strong and free?

Wanting to finish the journey wherever that may be

Would the solution I sought without success

Which led me to confusion and some distress

Be hiding somewhere in plain view

How to lift the blinders from my eyes and renew

Then it hit, how could I not see?

This new perspective lay not outside of me

No externals could help me find my way

My blind side spoke to me that day

Jung said many years ago

And though I'd read it, I failed to know

In looking outside one can only dream

Look inside and awaken to things yet unseen

It's hard to lift the rock that hides the key

Not out of fear but some outdated philosophy

When all along, there it lay

Then I knew this would be a new way

Am I sure now that I will find

That which will bring me peace of mind

No, I know Life offers no guarantee

But at least I can look with new visibility

I've learned many things along the way

With many more to learn before the end of my stay

And when face to face with a blank slate

When I've heaped high with all sorts my plate

If nothing works out as I'd hoped

I've done little more than coped

If a new adventure is what I need

Then I must change perspective and take heed

Readjust my astrolabe to guide me another way

From the short sightedness that led me thus astray

"**Mistakes are, after all, the foundations of truth, and if a man does not know what a thing is, it is at least an increase in knowledge if he knows what it is not.**"

C.G. Jung

THE WHAT OR THE WHY

October 2017

You may have noticed my interest in words. Each was born of a necessity to give a definite shape to our thoughts. They were given a precision in time and meaning, many empowered to fulfill different structural functions. They are the heart of our brain – think about that for a moment. Today we seem most concerned with the what – what we want, what we need, what makes us happy, what we want to do. I've noticed that when people are looking to mee, they often use the term "…seeing what's out there." I would have thought "who" would have been more appropriate, but I am mistaken. People no longer seem to want to find a "who," as that would engage them too deeply. Better to find a "what", based on a checklist of characteristics that is expected somehow to make one happy, while never being obliged to commit deeply. The "Who" is, of course, important. But underlying everything is the reason "why" we want what we want, why we make choices, why we choose one thing over another. There is a value system, a structure elaborated over time which, unconscious for the most part, which drives every aspect of our behavior. Ignore it, and someone else is driving the car. Reflect on it, and however much freedom we have as human being in our civilization – itself a debate I will not engage in here – we will always have more. Up to you.

The What or the Why

The ground or the sky

A natural pairing, they ally

No need so hard to try

The first is real

To touch and feel

Like the air we breathe. When we eat a meal

There for the taking, no need to steal

It's how we build our reality

What else exists that we don't see?

Its rules are simple and easy to apply

The more we have, the more we want to buy

-

From the earliest times before we could think

Really only it was what to eat and drink

Survival required no high mindedness

The world was then an most dangerous mess

At first defined by the concrete from which we came

The game was simple and had but one name

And what the name implied was always the same

Regardless the means, survive to stay in the game

Not down to the earth from which we came

Limited by definition, and always the same

Lift our regard up then to the sky, limitless and free

From there could come some answers, perhaps even clarity

And so began a journey into worlds immaterial

To bring a higher order and end the chaos serial

How did this happen, what gave us the key?

To look in new places, new possibilities to see

One word, so simple, three letters alone

Why is the beginning of all that has come to be known

It supports all things, bearing "whats" we never understood

And introduced the very human notions of bad and good

Curiosity, its motor, the need to know

Without it we only shrink as we cease to grow

New seeds go unplanted, fields left untilled

We take without thought and the rest is killed

So what has turned the ship around?

That now we are headed backwards, landward bound

Fearing the unknown, longing only for more

Who cares what's driving the ship or what's behind the door?

 see no good issue, as all things turn inward to what now is ours

As our numbers grow with no thought of the world that it sours

Wild species dwindle as our hunger the land devours

There will soon be no fields of wild flowers

All sacrificed to the wants of the here and the now

A day when there isn't enough, back to what will our heads bow?

When all that was precious is no more

When there is no hope with its name on the door

When the young cease to believe in endless tomorrows

Then will we see we've created a world of sorrows.

THE MANY FACES OF "C" – *side 1*

September 2017

This started off with a brief reflection on the myth vs. the reality of Capitalism. As I wrote, I became aware of other factors which belong to the Capitalism equation. I had been seized by the letter "C." Once I had finished with the negatives, I started to wonder what factors which exist in society and are there to bring balance to the equation. Once again, the letter "C" took hold of me. Perhaps the most import "C" is consequence, for making decisions without anticipating consequences ensures another "C" – catastrophe.

CAPITALISM

Capitalism is our system, we've married our fate to it

There have indeed been periods of great success, enough to qualify as a hit

But what of those periods, dark and full of pain

Where so many lost what they had, where there was no gain

Unemployment, bubbles, corruption run amuck

And all this talk of deregulation, as if slow and steady means we're stuck

And tales of growth unlimited, as if that were a worthy goal

When all such fantasies can but create a monster hole

So much talk of capitalism, of Friedman and his school

If it was all so clear, why then is there no golden rule?

No system by itself alone can offer true perfection

For it is people who compose it, and prone to dereliction

So until such time as we ourselves can improve how tend to act

There is no system in this world that can guarantee success –
and that's a fact

COMPETITION

Inherent to Capitalism is something we claim to admire

Alone among all economic forces, it is the most prolific
sire

But to thrive and reproduce in ways that never tire

Only the free market knows best, why do we then not
hire

Because it is a myth, a creation of pure fantasy

For one to win, many must lose, let's think on this more clearly

Now those who win, whether through luck or skill

Or smarts or timing or relentless will

If winning is the goal – losers there must be

Praise be to this market forever free

And who are the losers, false or real?

The system requires it so why anything should I feel?

Are they not much like you or me?

Since I won, better I must be

Is that correct, the right conclusion drawn?

Or have I bought into the system, a simple pawn?

If lose means what I think it does, a closer look is required

Before we sign the contract, and the system is truly hired

His competitor has garnered all the gains, he was left in
the dust

With only himself to blame – his life had all gone bust

Let's remove some layers and away the onion peel

Normal times are interrupted, the boat shifts from its
even keel

Consequences fall from all directions

Have we assembled the appropriate protections?

Or do we focus only on those who win?

And assume the losers are victims of some sin?

Turbulence the symptom, the cause some new deal

The ground may shift, fortunes shaken. This is for real

For an innovative product, something we've not seen
  before

Consumers rush to acquire it, pushing through the door

The merchant, thrilled, sees his shelves go bare

Vision paid off, forgotten is the care

New orders must be placed

Risk is thus rewarded, anxiety erased

Unless not "smart" enough to stock this thing, to await his fate

Regret will start to fill his heart for now he is too late

What of those older things, now an empty bust

Tossed or sold for little, or simply left to rust

The game is lost, he scored no points, what will become of him

Well, too bad, for that's the way – one must play to win

And those who made and sold that which no one wants to buy

Layoffs are coming down the pike, so to your jobs prepare to say goodbye

CONFLICT-

For competition is a polite way to call what really is a war

We all know war on conflict is based, we know what lies in store

It begins for no clear reason, other than to win

To enrich oneself beyond what one has, how can that be a sin?

In the absolute, why not, since when is less more?

It's just what happens in between we all tend to abhor

For what is gained comes not from thin air, from somewhere it is taken

In one way or another, the winner holds what belonged to another, newly forsaken

And if a clear victor emerges from this sanitized fight

Much like boxers landing punches, a left often follows a right

Striking back, as best one can, until one hits the floor

Unable to himself up, for he can take no more

Now that he has lost what he had, what is he to do?

Telephone his lawyer and see if he can sue?

Let's be real and wonder if a third way can be found

Could we conceive a system where both could stick around?

Why is it no one has thought of this today?

One that would foresee a loss and plan some new way

Is there truly nothing where two might collaborate and not compete?

Would it be possible if we just turned down a bit the heat?

COLLUSION

Inherent in competing, allies one must seek

Most often this occurs in secret, allowing no one else a peek

The goal, to gain advantage, victory to ensure

If winning is the only good, then alliances are good and pure

But once again – it's unavoidable – how can one win if the other does not lose

So colluding becomes a subtle game of how the winning ally to choose

Self-interests can overlap, at least on paper it seems

But what happens when two win, such is the stuff of allied dreams

Yet collusion has an underside, one should always hedge one's bet

Betrayal often plagues the game, a clean alliance has never been as yet

In the end what happens, some losers and those who won

Setting the stage for the next round, doesn't it sound like fun?

CORRUPTION

We say that all is fair in love and in war

Which means all rules are out the door

We all know what corruption means, it's everywhere you look

In some places it's hidden, in others an open book

We may pretend it's limited to times of necessity

Once the war is won, we'll just welcome back good old honesty

Are we kidding? Who believes that once a rule is broken

Unless there is some real sanction taken, disapproval is but token

So in the end, whenever that is, what is really undermined?

Is our ability to distinguish what is honest, fair and kind?

And as the victory celebrations follow on each other's heels

Bells are rung announcing the joy that "everyone" surely feels

And the dirty tricks we played to gain this holy prize

Has now assimilated us, and our morality cut down to size

CAPITULATION

Once the celebrations end and the monuments are built

Isn't it only natural that the losers should feel some guilt?

Might makes right, is that not our way

Like the free market, it must have its day

Or rather does a different emotion rise to take its place

For with defeat comes hardship, and the defeated rarely met with grace

The aftermath's stepchildren: Reconstruction, reparations, resentment

I wouldn't call this uplifting nor some source of contentment

Confusion, disarray, despair, envy and greed

Defeated populations first meal is defined, on themselves they tend to feed

And if they rise again, though not always the case

Guess what starts all over again – the infernal chase

For no party ever defeated accepts the loss with ease

Like a splinter under the skin, revenge is a mighty tease

So for a time all might look calm, let bygones go by the
way

Beware the opportunity arising, for the loser to have his
day

COLLAPSE

And in the end of this inferrnal round

Have we really progressed onto some newly sacred
ground?

Capitalism is its name

Or have we done the opposite, only raising the stakes of
the game

When Capitalism calls to compete, will we not hear its
sound?

Is this its home thought sacred ground?

For fame, for, glory, but most of all for greed

Have you any doubt where this will ultimately lead?

Am I merely dreaming, can we ever hope to learn

That pushing each other aside instead of each taking his turn

Leads nowhere but back to where we began

Have we stopped short in our thinking, doing less than we can?

Innovation thrives on finding that which is not yet born

So let's use some brainpower, before that which binds us all is definitively torn

SIDE 2

COURTESY

What is this thing that used to be?

Though held by rules, it made us free

A contradiction one might think

Yet without it we lurch towards the brink

Competition brings a friction of sorts

Leading to all kinds of torts

Committed as if the other didn't count

Step on each other for most any amount

Friction causes a heat with can ignite a holy blaze

Easy to get into, difficult to exit – a maze

What was needed was a lubricant to smoothe the way ahead

So instead of flames of conflict, there's room enough instead

COMPROMISE

Two minds never think the same

For reasons obvious, too many to name

When decisions require a match

The answer can be difficult to catch

How to bring two sides worlds apart

How to reach the truth lying deep in their heart

To see beyond my words alone

Is there some magical compromise gnome

Or rather, behind the face of these two

Lies hidden something unrealized, yet new

To think and feel, can it be so?

Together they reveal the answer to know

Understanding another point of view

Blending it with one's own, that's how we grew

Into something bigger, better than before

That's how we were able to walk together through the door

Not thinking in terms of what I might lose

Consider what could be gained if we choose

Not my way or yours, that stuck in the past

A time, as we all know, never can last

So reach for the future, make it your own

And for certain both parties will have more wise grown

COLLABORATION

A word used different meanings to express

One suggests more, the other less

Rather than argue which one is right

And end up with nothing, but a useless fight

Let's take the middle road, neutral at its best

And consider the root meaning. Will it pass the test?

Collaboration means working together towards a common goal

Not directly implied is an eventual toll

One group that might suffer as a consequence

Making confrontations angry and tense

There's a thought to consider in this spirit to begin

Must working together include an enemy, along with some potential sin?

Why not think it through before it starts

Identify and examine all of the parts

Build in the solution where the damaged are few

Where everyone gains, then stir well the brew

With all heats and minds then firmly on board

So much easier to move everyone in one direction, forward

CONSTRUCTION

When all of the "C's" come together as one

That's when it can begin, the fun

For working in concert, great things await

A belief in progress replaces hate

Thoughts of just "me" seem to disappear

And with them that most debilitating emotion – fear

Whether or citizens, united we stand

Centripetal forces by nature have come to banned

The power of positive, demonstrated in act

None can deny the potential, and that is a fact

COMPLICITY

A concept emotional, based on a union of sorts

Where a deeper understanding has no need of courts

The basic assumptions require no further discussion

The opposite I suppose of American and Russian

It's a place of validation, all parties can feel secure

The beyond the concept, the bond will endure

It's a good place to be where a future awaits

Trust can grow with no filter at the gates

And when one trusts, innocence can return

And minds open up, much more able to learn

If this can be, good times can return

And the troubled past can be left to burn

Be it love, politics, science or school

The field is open for no one who can trust gets taken for a
fool

CONNECTION

A term often mentioned in matters of the heart

A desire to bridge the gap that keeps us apart

Blamed by most on technology, at fault

As if by our phones we've been locked in a vault

A virtual space alluring at first

Has proven to be an enemy, among the worst

Who knew what was artificial could come to exist

But, consider that word too, and you'll know why we
missed

Technology is meant to help in our task

To carry our burdens and help when we ask

But once we grow lazy, delegating what's real

That's when artificial becomes a wall to what we feel

A connection is something coming from deep within

It is meant to be real, not some fantasy sin

There too, virtual artificiality

Has taken us to a place of superficiality

Quick, fun, hot and more

If not, who has the patience – such a bore

So we get what we bought, unhappy it seems

Take me back, please, to my place of dreams

But reality takes time, effort and trust

So hard, all these things, are they really a must?

Let's put it this way, it's a simple choice

Know first who you are and speak with a clear voice

If you have ever known a connection that was real

One that took time and effort to grow and feel

Then you will know, it's the only thing that can endure

Fantasy can be fun, but it can't ever be pure

Be mindful of facts which on words are built

If you want quick and easy, fantasy comes with guilt

Constantly changing, the playground of the mind

There to imagine, not live, alone with no human kind

Connection is real, designed to last

It goes deeper, not wider, taking time, never fast

CONSIDERATION

This word is a favorite of mine

It expresses a way to live that I think is fine

Aside from the emotional piece, empathy engaged

One must also use one's mind to see in some future
undefined yet staged

For of all the words I've looked into above

This one is necessary for us to experience love

It requires we think in present and future tense

An notice at all times, others with little pretense

I am no more important that you by any measure that counts

In human terms, our differences to very little amounts

So when living in spaces restricted or large

Try and remember to consider and not charge

Frictions occur, no need to heat them more

Others may be rushing to get through the door

Lubrication exists, consideration first among equals

`No use to live prequels, good to avoid sequals

`The present counts, make it easier for all

Lack in consideration and look small

Use your mind and your heart – a good reason to stand tall

For it determines if together we will stand or we'll fall

COMPASSION

Herein lies the glue that holds it all

Like a electricity, it flows and cannot stall

It's a magnet the way we to each other we are bound

A fundamental silent value, making not a sound

But hear its voice, no need to withhold

When we need each other, all become bold

Intolerable, we can sense, the pain others fee

How natural it is to want them to heal

Natural in the absolute, no need to teach

Where there is a need, we simply reach

What would the world look like if this were the case

If compassion was to politics our new home base?

No need to fear we might give it all away

For those we've helped will respond if ever might come such a day

There you go, both sides of the "C's."

I don't know where it came from, it just grew like some trees

Tall and strong, with a message that's clear

I followed its call with little or no fear

And here's we've landed, for those brave enough to endure

Just another way to think about how it might feel on our return from the cure

ONE THING AT A TIME

December 2017

*An old theme, exposed by many, so then why does it keep getting worse? Why all this pointless rushing which creates a sense of self-importance through busyness? Perhaps the reason is that no one really thinks much anymore, asks themselves important questions, believes that they might *actually be able to have an impact. If these things are absent, if you fill your head with noise, which is little more than distraction, listening to other people's opinions so you don't have to develop your own, then ask yourself one simple question: who really runs my life?*

Have you noticed of how people scurry?

Rushing everywhere, always in a hurry

Complaining of all they have to do

To any who would listen, the many or the few

Never asking the importance of things

Just line up the tasks and wait till the bell rings

When the race begins, a brand new day

I just don't see how it's worth it to live this way

There is, of course, a hierarchy real

Based on externals, there is a deal

Look outside, embrace the rules

Seems to me, we've just become tools

Grateful for the distraction, no questions one need ask

Just pile them up, keep my time filled with every task

Rush home, what a day I had

So much done, so why am I sad?

Was anything real accomplished at work?

My personal life has suffered, am I a jerk?

For we rush around, from here to there

You know what's missing/– knowing when to care

With no idea of what really is real

For me or anyone else, I'm no longer sure how to feel

Not some passing pleasure, some intense sensation

Once it's gone, I notice its short duration

Stop then and think, listen to what's wrong

Turn off your music, forget that song

For what you do, though you blame the tech

It just fills your head with senseless noise, and leaves you a wreck

How to have any chance of ever finding what's real?

If you've forgotten to discover what's important, and how it makes you feel

Alive, with direction, why you are here

And a reason to stand up for something without any fear

TIRED

November 2017

What happens when certain subjects become designated as "to be avoided," issues," to be stored and never discussed. Most frequently it is between parents and children, when the child's personality and interests start to distinguish themselves from the family value system. Parents tend to think of children as extensions of themselves, rarely recognizing the individual this child is destined to become. When a parent sees a child deviate from the family culture, rather than understand that it's a sign of growth, they become disappointed, even disillusioned, saying to themselves they don't know what happened to their child, they weren't like that before, etc., etc..A battle for one's soul is engaged, and depending on the strength and convictions of each, how much they are capable of letting go their hold on each other, life gets stuck, and the relationship – even if seemingly good growing up – becomes a struggle for Independence, , even identity. Why "Tired?" Because it's exhausting and a war that rarely ends.

Tired I grow, trying to explain

Where we have gone wrong in our own domain

Life can be complicated, often we make it so

There are means to come to know

Oneself, the center from which we came

Before we ever had a name

Before others began to mold

And our true path began to grow cold

Can a future really be sold?

And if it is, does it make us old?

Yet somehow it can never disappear

Its call remains though neither loud nor clear

Abandonned perhaps, never forgotten

Who can live a life too misbegotten?

A mask is sculpted from many a compromise

In the moment, perhaps a solution wise

As time passes, as it's worn each day

It start to take hold in a subtle way

The more time spent living a life not our own

Who is living? Who is known?

Do they know where they are going or by which wind
they are blown?

Have the seeds they planted ever grown?

In the place of a face, a mask is worn

Designed not to be real, but to adorn

The more its worn, the further we stray

The core, the essence begins to fade away

Never unfamiliar, it's who we are

Estrangement, however, raises the bar

The distance between them grows too far

Doubt takes hold, and obscurs the North Star

Search we may for means of release

Moments of calm, but no inner peace

Back to where it all began years ago

When we relied on others, ourselves to know

For parents can be strict, seeing a child as their own

Deviate from their view and their ire will be known

Well meaning, for the most part

A child needs parents to learn a part

But will it be theirs after all the edits

Who deserves the failures and the credits?

If too great a divide is born

The fabric of the family is torn

A truce is found, a compromise

More is lost than gained, is that wise?

For in the heated crucible, temperatures will rise

The wounds are rarely healed, and the wound never dries

Rare are things brought into the purifying light

The thorns lying at the source are sent off into the night

Subjects difficult, never spoken

Something fundamental is now broken

A neutral zone, a place where nothing can grow

In the family plot, nothing now can grow

These zone of silence, where hurts are sent to die

Where healing talk cannot try

Denied entry, frozen in time

A buffet cold on which to dine

These are also the things of which lives are made

Too many end up stunted, the price they've paid

A tribute to the past, no debt ever forgiven

To break its hold, a stake must be driven

Through the very heart of those we're told to love

These old wound, we should rise above

Or so it's said from those who claim to be wise

How to cure if the infection one denies?

Time and again, these simple thoughts can be agreed

For a time, this way seems to meet a need

But touch that place, the nerve that's raw

Too often, we're lucky to get a draw

In these moments of conflicts intense

When the past lives again in the present tense

With no perspective, no growth, nothing has changed

If it escapes from its cage, all will be deranged.

No sunshine allowed to disinfect

No fresh wind some hope to resurrect

Both parties stuck, the stakes too high

To give an inch too hard to try

What a waste when time is short

When the only course seems to abort

And carry on one's solitary way

Living in limbo for yet another day

Or

Define the place where "I" begin

A part, yet distinct, from family and kin

as violent perhaps as when entering this world

Defenseless, dependent, in a ball shape, curled

The difference, of course, defenseless no longer

The years that preceded should have made your stronger

Taught by experience the courage required

How to extirpate oneself, not remain mired

In the emotions that a family define

Never to lose oneself, nor to resign

We get but one turn, though many phases there may be

Each bringing a lesson of how to be free

Some are learned, others deflected

Some walls are torn down – others resurrected

But in the end it comes down to one thing

Who will own your soul, what can it bring

The answer resides in the one you've become

No one else can determine if you've lost or won.

I preach this daily to friends in distress

Their lives too often in a mess

Denied as such until they can no more

Few listen, many head for the door

Strange how we embrace a powerless state

Conceding to other forces our future, our fate

Is it an illusion, the control we retain?

Is that why some speak of their mind instead their brain?

Perfect and happy – that's not what was ever intended

I doubt Life's Constitution will be amended

But as long as we see ourselves and feel alive

We are meant to struggle, to learn, to strive

Heroic perhaps this vision I maintain

Better to fight than stay on the train?

WHERE HIDES THE TRUTH

December 2017

As so often happens, I know where I start, but not where I'll end up. There are times when this is very frustrating, for I must struggle not just to evoke, but to be clear in a way that anyone – and not just me – can understand. This began as a concern as the truth is indeed under attack, and perhaps has been for sometime. We have always embraced lying as a legitimate defense, all the while praising, even teaching children, that they must always speak the truth – itself another lie, But what are the consequences as this convention gains explicit acceptance? They are many, they are grave, but the most frightening of all is the direction they take us all in. The Middle Ages were indeed a dark time, and nothing but ourselves and our will to be good stands in the way to their return.

Each life has a story with an internal coherence

Most don't see it, preferring the ease of ignorance

For consistency serves a different master

From the back of our minds he calls and we go faster

His role is drive efficiency

Time is money – don't you see?

What other word defines success so completely?

Afrer all, success will make us all happy

What is the nature of these efficiencies we seek

Look behind the heading and have a peek

What appears of insufficient use can be dismissed

If the goal is to always be the one first finished

If something is always lost when something is gained

What might that be, if on that day it rained?

Could we have learned some insight non-essential

Who cares if knowledge is no longer preferential

The focus was on this singular thing

All resources were focused, our energies did we bring

All together pushing to finish first

That must be good, but could it also be the worst?

The steps we skip like a hurried meal

Or the thoughts set aside, precious time will they steal

Are never digested, nor nourish our soul

In every way poorer, that is the toll

Life is complex, ever changing, yet we strive to know

Until recently, at least I think that it was so

It takes time to live, to experience the journey

What happens if we just gorge ourselves, and of digestion, never worry?

Whether mind or stomach, it's but an intermediate stage

Yet it is what happens therein that set out how we will age

Rush through it all, and little will remain

Incomplete digestion becomes the source of much pain

 Of the stomach, the heart, the mind and the soul

 For after all, together they work to make us whole

Stepping back now to examine the reason we are here

Are there other factors at play that might make us fear?

If what we are after is to know what is real

Then the time spent in reflection, provides time to heal

Why then do we use any reason large or small?

To avoid reflecting, our minds to stall

To silence our hearts, so they make no sound

Only material things provide us now with solid ground

What is solid, however, exists only in the present

It cannot transcend time and space, it is quickly spent

What can last, only limited by our attention

What can bind us together? is there some convention?

Not one of the mind, reason can justify all things

It may cover the surface, but its truth too often hollow rings

What keeps the departed always present and felt?

What spans generations, the God to whom all have knelt?

The force that binds, the glue cosmic

Is what allows to choose, allows us to pick

Because of its force, we can take a stand

Life finds significance and guides our hand

Though it can serve evil or good

To be sure, on need look under the hood

For those with the courage and curiosity

It's right there waiting for us to see

Reality will always be colored by subjective vision

It's the closest we can get to any clarity of vision

Aware and alert, honest and prepared

All brought together, from many tragedies we can be spared

But for those who know this yet choose what's unreal

Find the image they see in the mirror unfamiliar so they seek to steal

Something that's safe, unthreatening is best

To live on the margin, hiding from themselves and the rest

If this is indeed who we have become

If fear has ousted courage, and the many want a gun

When ignorance has chased knowledge leaving no place to pause

Then where can truth live, if indeed this was the cause

If our culture prefers to ignore

With some new construct has the truth well hidden behind a locked door

Then the road ahead grow darker, the future dissolves

Fear now the motor around which mankind revolves

Demons inhabit this world dark and drear

Clarity the enemy, one we fear

How odd to live ignoring the most obvious of things

Even our language speaks of gorillas in the room and naked kings

How did this happen and why is it so?

Is there an answer that we can know?

The first thought lights on concordance of views

Its safer to repeat than to learn from the news

Is it sloth then the answer, the reason for denial

Are we just to lazy to defend ourselves at our own trial?

And what of pure evil, its minions abound?

Is not the denial of truth a lie with no sound?

And finally, conflict, the most obvious cause

Inconsistencies reveal our most painful flaws

All together prevent us from having a point a view

One informed with some merit, possibly even new

To have a point of view, the result of experience and reflection

Incontrovertibly points us in a specific direction

For to have a true thought, if thoroughly done

Represents a step forward, not some game that we've won

Though too many see our system with its many "C's"

Require some form of conflict, and not to please

Confrontation means simply two forces that meet

More often adversarial, a strenuous feat

One then has two choices, the most determinant of all

To silence oneself, of to defend the call

Of the truth, or perception, or whatever you prefer

To say yes to oneself, and step forward, one cannot defer

To do so would negate a part of our personal lives

Making us smaller and of no consequence – defeatism drives

And to go with the flow, repeating without thought

In truth, what has one thusly bought?

In all things one has turned away from ones core

If you observe carefully, you will see the closing of mind's door

Letting nothing in, and nothing out

I wonder with what they fil their heads, what's that about?

And how then to choose one path or another

Confusion reigns where there was no father or mother

To point out the roads of right and wrong

Such is the foundation lives are built upon

If parents don't defend in seriousness this vital precep

How can the children even guide their lives knowing only "except"

A reference to their individuality, inflated beyond recognition

Yet really on superficially, for no depth has been given

It is what it is. I'm not in the mood

Let's not think of dinner – just call out for food

Facility. Ease. Too much choice

Stupidity. Avoidance. Only opinion has a voice

A sad picture have I painted – reflecting years of observation

And what it has done to this once great nation?

One final thought on two words often used though not the same

Judgmental, a horror, dismissive and lame

Designed to disqualify any critical thought

In its downward spiral have we not been caught?

A moral imperative being its implication

No thought is given to its justification

God forbid that we take a stand

Defending intelligent convictions should be banned

Observation – a word more empirically based

No snap judgements to conclusions should be traced

Engage in life, feed you mind

Live by your values and be kind

Fail in this, from nowhere expected will appear a slow leak

Which cannot but empty your heart and make you weak

Truly dark times once existed and for centuries lasted

Poverty, war and disease and for years people fasted

Not enough of anything to make a life of peace

It can return again if the dark forces yet again we release.

FOUND IN THE LAND OF THE LOST

January 2018

I've often asked myself a very fundamental question, one I think we all implicitly consider from childhood on. It derives from the notion of reward: if I do the right thing, will things necessarily turn out well? Of course, the basic assumption is also true for the opposite. The relationship to parental authority, transferred later to social institutions, themselves rooted in some higher spiritual power, should be evident. But there is a third way which only experience confronts us with. It is the fact that very often – too often some might say – we do the right thing and the only reward we have is to know that we did the right thing to the best of our abilities. This is, of course, the eternal dilemma, i.e. that evil exists in the world. In this poem, I look at it from a slightly different angle. I have spent much of my life defining a set of values that I believe in, that can guide me. But the reward is not something external to myself. It is the belief that in so doing, I become more consequential, most consistent, and more coherent. The benefits would be to make me a more sincere, caring, trustworthy, reliable man, a devoted father, and someone who sees himself attempting to make a contribution. This doesn't derive from any nobility, but rather the conviction – based on observation and experience – that this is the path that has revealed itself to me. So where is the reward? Basically, as Jung said, "....the greatest privilege in life is to become oneself." This isn't an endorsement of selfishness, but rather a weighty responsibility, an obligation to oneself and one's peers. No! Good and Evil exist in some absolute form (though I am fairly certain that Evil exists in concrete form, whereas Good is an ideal, an aspiration, and therefore more of a spiritual nature), as do right and right and wrong. Not because someone has taught us. Rather this is what Life has revealed to us. And what has also become apparent is the necessity for some clarity, some stability, some moral sense to provide structure and purpose to society, and to hold at bay the forces of darkness, and their most potent ally, relativization. Having lived in many different cultures, I have come to see the absurdity of absolutes and the cruelty of living in a world where everything can, and should, be explained away, more as convenience than necessity. Am I right in so many ways? Are my peers wrong in just as many? I don't think so. What I do believe is that I have found a certain center, while those I see everyday, have come to resemble discrete systems unto themselves, the insufficient relatedness to others is its most marked symptom. That is a serious threat to us all.

As I've wandered the world in search of some truth

I've run the gamut from smooth to uncouth

Though the former is more my element of choice

We all net to test our wills and our voice

There have been moments when doubt took hold

And I always knew when I was getting too bold

Knowing when the experiment was done

And it was time to walk away intact, rather than run

Convention has mostly ruled my space outside

At times I felt my truth I needed to hide

But then I came to a startling conclusion

I owned myself and that was no illusion

No need to share every aspect to all

I never returned the "in your face" call

Something I knew would watch over me

And alert me to dangers that I did not see

So though there have been missteps, some major at
times

I've managed to make sense of most, oddly in rhymes

For I think it's not all me that writes this verse

It comes to me spontaneously, I never rehearse

I feel connected when others hear what I share

Some of it universal, some personal that I dare

But knowing most pay little heed

To fear some reaction, there is little need

I've landed back in the place where I began

Often on my own with no need of a fan

Wondering at times if too self-sufficient I've grown

If that's the case it's due to what I have known

The years we are given to learn what Life is about

The challenges and hardships to burn the
imperfections out

Those doubts that haunted our earlier years

Those demons who whispered inside of our ears

That chip on our shoulder, mother of all mistakes

Has lessened its grip, my decisions it no longer makes

One might think, what a life awaits

He can probably even catch of those pearly gates

Not so, no the road was not built for ease or reward

It's there so continue our long march forward

Now if you've read this far and haven't lost interest yet

With no details, only allusions, that' a pretty good bet

After painting a picture that was all about me

Confident, secure, but sure not all I can be

For the rest of the picture, the part that's incomplete

Is the rest of the world, and what happens when our
values meet

Having lived in two worlds, so different at heart

I have written by myself, the lines to my own part

But that tells me, I've failed to learn others

Back home after so long, I have little in common with
sisters   and brothers

So, If I am found must the others be lost

Have I managed to pay a different cost

Would a return to where all those years were spent?

Would I feel more at home in that foreign tent?

Or have I become the fruit of some universal tree

The one where each one is as different as can be

Their common parent unites them all

In ways fundamental, but practically, rather small

Each fruit, when it falls, lands where it may

Unique for sure, though unable to live in the same way

As those who inhabit the place where he lives every day

To work, to think, to help, to speak and to play

At ease, enjoying random talk, even jokes

One might easily think he's just one of the folks

Being part from here and part from there

He is both everywhere, yet belonging nowhere

So there you go – a formulation new

Has my question come full circle or hopefully grew?

So many words, so much noise these reflections make

Sometimes I wonder if too much time do they take

Then I remember it's not me who gets to decide

When one feels lost, it best to hand over the reins and enjoy the awhile the ride.

TECHNIFY

December 2017

The past several years have revealed a very clear tendency, a shift in our fundamental beliefs, away from our human ability to solve problems, towards a longing for some superior technology, almost a God-like figure – that, thanks to its superior intelligence, will solve problems for us. Supporting this trend is a marked interest in all things technical where we assign an independent existence and identity to our favorite, and fast evolving gadgets where they become more than tools of productivity or convenience. They become real. Is this being driven by a certain lazyness on our part, a lassitude of having to work so hard to solve problems – many of them seemingly beyond our ability to resolve? This fatigue leads us to delegate more and more of that which brought us to where we are today – a native curiosity, an innate striving.. A bit of a conundrum. Science fiction has theorized that the machines would one day turn against us. I fear rather that we will turn against ourselves only to embrace something we created, some false ido. But on the way, will we not have quantified, technified every endeavor, every solution so as to be able to return to a somewhatchildlike state of dependence where only futile pursuits would be capable of garnering our attention? Look around you. Listen to the discourse where intelligent – though non-thinking (in my opinion) invoke Artificial Intelligence, "the brain," hard wiring, neuro-chemistry in ways that may appear knowing and considered, when in fact, they are empty prayers to empty gods Is it our destiny to come full circle?

Here's a word you may not know

It's a verb, an action word whose use may grow

Invented to express a thought

For something by which we have been caught

It starts with technology

A truth at first, now a tautology

An absolute, the One will save us all

From what? Itself perhaps, if we don't get too small

And the second part, what does it imply?

A transformational word that isn't shy

Together they take something real

Something we can touch and feel

Something that has an existence of its own

Something so familiar, we all have known

And then we give it technical spin, how its then grown

Into a new marvel, changing the tone

Of whatever it was we were talking about

And along the way, it's acquired more clout

Now let's take an example, something we can explore

And hopefully on the way, learn so much more

How about doctors their pains and their woes?

For they must endure so much so their knowledge grows

Learning physiology, etiology, pharmacology and more

Hoping this will suffice for what's in store

Over dinner with a good friend gynecologist

She told me of the weight they carry until I got the gist

For according to her, they face life and death every day

Without saying it – becoming God-like that way

Technology comes first, new methods all the time

The doctor-patient relationship no longer fine

Rush, rush, rush, can't really talk

Diagnose, treat, bill – then out the door – walk

Lost somehow they've come to feel

Odd for a profession whose goal is to heal

So what do they do for there is a need?

Whose advice might they seek out and heed?

None other than other doctors who believe

That only another doctor from this pain can relieve

More of the same? Is that really the solution?

At best it's talking to oneself – at best a dilution

How about groups to talk this through?

Reserved for doctors, what else is new?

So there you are, a solution self-defined

Was that what they had from the start in mind?

All pieces to their simplest expression reduced

Build on the obvious, analyzed, deduced

A process, bigger than what came before

Less never works, we must always have more

I could go on, but I think you now see

What's wrong with this solution? Can it be?

How they've reduced themselves through "operationality"

Cogs in a machine, plying their trade but unhappy

Emptied of substance, nothing there to assuage

This is the malady infecting our age

For we have technified what once was natural

Making things too concrete can be counterfactual

Instead of learning to look within

A different perspective could bring a win

At the very least, enlightened by the contrast

Some benefit could come, and might even last

We are humans, made of flesh and blood

With flaws and qualities mixed in with some mud

But that's who we are, that's where we must look

Not everything can – nor should – be done by the book

But if doctors train doctors, that's all that they know

How beyond technology can they ever grow?

All lose this way, the impureties burned away

From where will come new ideas, pleasure and play

This is true for us all as technology continues to eat us alive
It's not bad, in fact it can help us live and thrive

It's only when it becomes a God in our mind

That the threat becomes real to all humankind

Stop seeking perfection thinking to transform humans into machines

And it does matter by which means

Do you not see what this might mean in the end?

And to our children, what message does this send?

To grow up in a world where the machine is a hero

Leaving us supporting roles, our value declining to zero

Without us to guide them, what values would they hold?

They'd see us as imperfect, and one day grow bold?

Not a new vision of some dark future, we've seen before

But let's not rush to open that door

Speed, efficiency, – qualities machines have for sure

Would it not be better if we are to endure?

To expand our own qualities, the wonders that await

A better idea perhaps. Let's not wait.

THE PLACE WHERE I GO

October 2017

We all have our moments of weakness and abandonment when there is something which beckons to us, promising relief, but in the end, at a terrible cost. Be it alcohol, drugs, sex, gaming, etc.. These are dangerous places, tempting, seductive, offering temporary relief. Go if you must. But if you are ever to return home, keep in touch with yourself always. These are places where the center of your being resides. We all need where to look up at the sky to find our North Star.

There is a place I always go

When something is wrong and I don't know

Which way to turn, which choice to make

So my faith in what's right I don't forsake

Two lines simply enter my head

And so it begins, the answer is said

The answer can be easily read

And with that, I can go peacefully off to bed

But now, a fog has descended, no clarity to find

Though I've defined each piece in my mind

I could try and write myself a letter in prose

Not knowing why, my heart has otherwise chose

How can I tell? It's so easy to see

I can sit down and write, and for awhile, maybe

An answer takes shape, coalescing until I realize

I've gotten lost and the matter I must resize

So unfinished, I set the piece aside

Embarrassed, disappointed that I could f not to hide

From myself, for this is what it means

I can be led astray by myself into many scenes

Why is this so? What's prevents me from knowing?

The reasons why I seem to have stopped growing

Part of the answer is a crutch that I've found

A surrogate for the things I needed that were not around

And as so often happens – I predicted it before

Frustration was waiting behind the door

"Better than nothing" was my rationalization

Like everyone else in our self-deluding nation

Yet all along I knew the dead end it was destined to be

But as long as it provided some distraction and company

It didn't take long to discover why they kept on coming

For they too, the experience was momentarily numbing

Until I could no longer refuse to see

They came for other reasons than to be with me

I know this now, there's escape

It's as if I'd confessed it all and kept the tape

But during these few years when it filled a void

It changed the nature and may very well have destroyed

That which it was supposed to sustain

And of those who filled my time, almost none remain

Yet I continue on this road to nowhere

It's easy, so why should I care?

People matter less, though I know it's not right

And yet it regrows, this caring, so why fight?

So here I am, rather stuck and rendered blind'

Where this new door can I find?

My heart speaks but the world doesn't seem to care

I retreat back into my lair

I write to understand, thinking a solution might exist

I don't know how to give in, so I continue to resist

None are immune to the prevailing ways

One can try to stand firm through all of the days

But sooner or later, frustration sets in

And I embrace once again, this friendly sin

I am not made of facile stuff

I've learned in life one must ride out the times rough

It's taken me a lifetime to get where I am

I will remain vigilant, perhaps build a dam

One that will keep me safe from intoxication

There are better ways to deal with this nation

Who am I kidding, that's no solution

The answer lies in one's own resolution

It must for me alone, by myself be done

For the man I am today, and was always meant to become

No admonition, not threat of any kind

Could separate me from this thing now living in my mind

I am strong, I know how to leave

 I won't miss it at all, nor will I grieve

But those who indulge have proven one point

Once their high priest, only he can anoint

Like any belief, his power derives

From the many stories, fictions and lies

Your soul you may give away

If you listen to him, and his orders obey

Hold on to your mind, your heart knows the way

Back to your home, and just maybe, a new day

But give yourself away to a power greater than you

Without fail, it will own you, and exact its due

THE OTHER FOUR LETTER WORD

NOVEMBER 2017

A riddle of sorts, though not very difficult, an example of how little words carry so much meaning. And along with their meaning, they can alter almost any choice one might need to make. See how quickly you find it.

It all comes down to one simple thought

With one simple word, the world can be bought

For through these four little letters we pick and choose

Who will win and who will lose

They guide us in ways we rarely consider

As thoughtlessly we concede the pot to the highest bidder

Leaving on the table the need to think

Is it wine or hemlock we're about to drink?

Was it always so hard to ponder our choices?

Simpler to follow the loudest voices

The words that were spoken, lost in the din

To support or oppose some collective sin

Something that lay dormant, a thought of little concern

Until the fire was fed, hotter to burn

And as the temperature climbed along with the flame

Out of the inferno an image came

Something to unite us and drown those dissenting souls

The masses lined up gladly to labor like mindless trolls

Why bother with details, flaws in the plan?

To march in unison each woman, every man

Believing some truth had newly been born

Displacing what came before, so tired and worn

And so it goes until it can go no more

Those details proven obstinate, impossible to ignore

Like some infection, they grow from within

Draining the force from the prevailing sin

Is there a cure or at least a vaccine?

Capable of protecting our exceptional team

It's hard to say, for once lost, it's hard to find

A fundamental shift has seized control of our mind

For together we may march, believing all is well

Unconcerned for the story history will tell

The letters? What are they, or have you guessed?

If so, then you may have indeed been blessed

Though being good at guessing games, however fun

Will never be able to bring back the Sun

No, it's of *caring* that I speak

I know – now six letters – I sprung a leak

Or rather imply to care, what does it mean?

And how did it ensure the dream?

To care is no simple emotion

It implies so much more, like devotion

And what of loyalty, spanning time

And respect for thinking – yours and mine

To care about all that came before

When making plans, consequences one does not ignore

To speak, mindful of how one's words one does hear

With clarity, conviction, consequence, but not fear

Games have no place, they intention often to mislead

Sowing confusion, mistrust and competition they breed

To have a stake in this one life we are given

By things other than money and power are we driven

To care means to know what one might lose

To think with emotion, so much better will we choose

GIVERS AND TAKERS

January 2018

A playful reflection on a distinction that we all make, where too often both parties feel wronged. At that point, if there is not some new perspective on the "what" and the "wh"y two people chose each other – whether it be for the "right" or "wrong" reasons (whatever they are) – there is a way forward. Why playful? Because without humor, there is rarely any productive perspective on oneself.

There are those who give and those who take

It's an old story but let's see if I can remake

The way we view the how and the why

It's important, so let's give it yet another try

Let's start at the point of emptiness

It's normal for those who feel they have less

To want more, having less is a pain

It's unfair to those deprived and they want to gain

But how does that happen, by birth or by luck?

When opportunity flew by, did they go for it or duck?

And what of those who want to give?

It's almost vital for them, they need it to live

Do they have a precondition, some requirement to be met?

How did it come about that they were able to more get?

Born to good fortune, be it family, talent or fame?

Were they smarter and knew how to pick the right game?

All of this can be true, there is no single rule

It's time to get wet so let's jump in the pool

Starting with the takers, let's narrow the scope

How about something easy like love and hope?

The theory goes that to give love one must have received

The same goes for hope, if it is to be believed

Pushing on, these good things that come our way

For sufficient quantities, it takes more than one day

So multiple times, while growing up

Someone was there to fill the cup

Next question then, can such bounty be stored?

And does it grow by itself when one feels adored?

At what point does it dawn on us there's pleasure to give?

And why is it vital for them to give

Once the transfer begun, is the balance drawn down?

Is there a point at which the smile becomes a frown?

Or rather is it a phenomenon unique?

Let's continue on and have another peek

It's said that love, once expressed grows over time

Infinite quantities can flow like wine

As long as the receiver grows like a plant in the sun

There is no end to the joy and the fun

So there we are, something than can't run out

Though unlike rivers, it must flow in both directions,
that's what it's about

Now what of the takers, what makes one of these?

In many ways they are like givers, they too want to
please

They give in ways that may look the same

But something is off in their way, their game

Their gifts come with strings, never free of charge

They too have hearts, but they smaller, not large

Or perhaps were they cracked, vessels that leak?

Here too, let's go deeper and take another peek\

Assuming they've not lived in the sun

A darkness always present, and most likely less fun

Were conditions more harsh, parents themselves
deprived?

A heavy legacy to carry, though they have survived

Their cup remains lacking, be it in function or fill

Life has taught them of limits, be careful not to spill

To waste what is precious, when there was never enough

When essentials are lacking, life can become tough

The less is felt like a hole in the gut

It can too often feel like living in a rut

They've given before, everyone tries

Too often they were met with betrayal and lies

Through some choice unfortunate, or perspective unclear

Less came back than was given, what remained was too dear

No evidence came either of this source without end

If not replaced automatically, best what remains to defend

A dilemma for sure, can one live without?

And that's how a new strategy came about

If some have enough, even more than they need

If they have more when they give, there can be no greed

But if you are lacking, and hunger for more?

There is one solution and comes with an easily opened door

One needs to give, the other wants to take

A marriage made in heaven, a cake ready to bake

But let's not forget the condition required

It must flow in both directions, or things get mired

The giver senses something is missing, something is wrong

They may have the music, but they hear no song

Ignorant through innocence, no less of a fault

They assume the takers are like them, not hiding a vault

A place where to hide the stolen treasure

To take all that they can, without any measure

The lines are now drawn, the problem not set

Not all of the conditions have been satisfactorily met

The givers withdraw, closing the tap

The takers must find a way to force open again the gap

Deception, guilt, manipulation of all sorts

Suddenly this love is covered with warts

And so it goes, how givers and takers compose

Some will endure, no love here grows

Others will try, mostly the givers for they can

Leave and look elsewhere, be they woman or man

How does it end? It's a riddle for sure

There are no givers or takers that are entirely pure

Blind they are, unless they have seen

Just how unsuspecting they have been

Takers seek out givers, though none carry the name

The givers need some wounded heart to tame

To shower with love, thinking only to heal

All the takers need do, is open their hearts and feel

More easily said than readily done

How to open one's heart when growing up with no Sun?

Is there no answer to this frightful scene?

If no remedy is found, both will grow mean

It requires great courage, for one must face

The pain that has lived in darkness complete

Reach out to it, love it, chronic hunger is not easy to defeat

The wind always blows cold, it brings no heat

Some wounds are too deep they can never heal

All they know is pain, like an old friend they can feel

But those who dare, and find ways to care

Life may not be perfect, but it will become more fair

And what of those lucky ones, whose hearts are full

Their merit is no greater, time to lift the wool

They've been in love with their ignorance for way too long

It's time to see that things are not that simple, to belong

To love another one must love oneself a bit less

Accept to get dirty and help clean up the mess

If not, if their perfection always comes first

Then the pressure to give will build, their loneliness the worst

Life can be cruel, challenges abound

We do have a choice, if we listen to the sound

And see what's clear, it's right before our nose

But if we don't look up, all we'll see are our toes.

STASIS

October 2017

After a divorce one faces many decisions, most notably where to live. Should one strike out on a new adventure, entering the unknown but taking a real chance for success. Or, should one stay close to home, to what is familiar. The reasons for either can be expressed simply: it all comes down to what one wants from life. Want more and risks are required. Accept less, and the future will most likely look very much like the past. It's a turning point in life when one can see of exactly what one is made. And at a vulnerable time. But there it is – believe in an a yet unwritten future where one enters the unknown with no guarantee of success. Or, embrace security and familiarity along with the loss of a chance at more. Which would you choose?

Life is force that can't stand still

It's at its best when going up or down a hill

The worst place to be is stuck somewhere

For that's where it's hardest to know what to dare

No direction is clear, no purpose at hand

One looks around with no idea where to stand

All things seem pointless, energy drains

People lose their minds speaking only of their brains

Am I but an organ, no longer master of my fate?

A mass of connections where I hardly rate

Drowning in a complex chemical bath

When did I lose my own path?

But I am not one of those

Vigilant, I always chose

In younger days, the future called

Open fields did I see, no city walled

Yet comes a time when the shape of things

Spinning out of control, no longer concentric rings

The children leave us to discover what is no more

What to do when each other we bore?

Go begin a life again we are told

Embrace the future and be bold

Many consider it, but few are sold

Courage fades as we grow old

Not for me, here I stand

In the city of my birth in my native land

Returned to my vocation that I left for a while

Wiser and older, but with the same style

What would that be, this thing called style

Begin with a faith in the future and an appropriate smile

A willingness to engage. Why be alone?

And an openness, inviting others to be known

Armed this way, I jumped back into the stream

Somewhat disillusioned, but still with a dream

So what is missing, where to find?

Another of a similarly curious mind

Who feared not to know of what we are made

And found their center, no longer waylaid

Whose life has known ups and its downs

Whose smile returns nonetheless to chase the frowns

Thirty years is a very long time

Cultures change including mine

A mix of Europe and the New York Jew

There are many of each, but of both very few

Excuses are easily found, most shun the blame

But I fear not, honest mistakes carry shame

To find the answer, one must look

Sometimes in places not recommended in the book

But never alone, one eye always on my North Star

Keeping close to my path so I strayed not too far

We each write alone, our story, our book

Much can be learned if we but take a good look

Each life is a story, revealed over time

And the narrative has a very clear line

When but one write the story, complications decline

When two join together, there's a yours and a mine

The equation is shared, neither must resign

Together decide that things will be fine

With will and intention, possibilities exist

When old wounds are left behind, there's little reason to resist

To build a future, a shared vision required

And with caring to ensure neither will be fired

Look back to know how one arrived here today

Understanding what the past has to say

Opens the road to the future, the way

Armed with the knowledge, our role we could play

Molding the future, sticking close to our core

Coherence and clarity opened many a door

No guarantee of success is ever given

But from our homes, no longer were we driven

I alone write the thoughts that become my book

For I know where I traveled and how long it took

If the other did as much, and owns their life

Maybe there will be a place for a new wife

Each chooses their way, up or down

To follow life's current or stay in town

Yet what to do when the current stalls

And it's vitality goes still as the energy falls

Left floating midstream, no direction clear

Uncertain of my way but feeling no fear

Unless this stasis should endure

For among all things, boredom has no real cure

Look outside and drown in a flood of noise

Distraction abounds along with the toys

Look inside and find new substance, clarity awaits

Yet what I see at present are only closed dates

So there you are, that's what lies within view

Have I played my last card, are my options so few?

Before I chose to cast a wide net

Thinking in numbers was my safest bet

So many in my life have come and left

Some gave me treasure, most turned to theft

Stubborn is my nature so I stay the course

Too long have I waited before changing my horse?

Instead of numbers, true prospects I seek

If instead of the strong, I find mostly the weak

Move on, for who named me healer to the needy

For they come to take, not give, too often just greedy

Beyond this point the fog is thick

I must wait and be thankful for not being sick

It's the hardest thing for me to do

As I wait impatiently to meet that someone new

CAN THE WELL RUN DRY?

August 2017

We rarely think about what might happen if the proper functioning of society were to hit a wall, preferring to focus on the present, until and unless otherwise required. We simply choose not to think about it, or rationalize it away, usually by deferring any action which would require a sacrifice of comfort or convenience in the present.   And when it happens……These concerns generally relate to nfinancial or environmental matters, but what about emotional matters? What might the world look like if we became so self-centered, so socially disconnected that empathy was no longer an option and we found ourselves in a place where we will have depleted all reserves of caring through the abusive us of the "transactional" model. It all come down to caring – about ourselves, each other, our institutions, lesser creatures, and the world which has harbored us, nurtured us since we crawled out of the swamp.   So take a moment to consider what is precious, what is fragile, and then do what is necessary to ensure its survival. Nourishi t so that it may not only flourish but in so doing, it will banish the darkness which drives us to ignore what holds everything together – our ability to care. It too can be lost – maybe even forever.

In this place where dark forces rule

Children of the light often feel the fool

Theirs is a way to make them whole

It's for real and not some empty role

Though manifest, yet never planned

They've learned to be alive one must take a stand

Not for some altruistic ideal of old

For authenticity's sake, one must be bold

Innocence. Naivete. Faith and Hope

These are the forces to battle the dark, and cope

The y come from deep within, a well

When in need, the waters begin to swell

Yet every well goes only so deep

Too many trips and the water advance but at a creep

For what was meant to never run dry

As long as it never had to hear the lie

The one that's told when lovers mislead

Silently, the heart knows and begins to bleed

This pump residing in out chest

Is not immune when put to the test

The wealth that comes from deep inside

When too often mocked thinks but to hide

Abandoning its task, the pump of life

It feels as if into its core was plunged a knife

By too much darkness it can be killed

What else can fill its chambers and see it thrilled

A reason to pump, its purpose willed

No longer rise the waters, no vessel filled

To drain a heart of its treasure, to take it all

Like vampires, would cast a lethal pall

The light too, the one that makes daytime bright

An ally must come and join the fight

For the dark forces arrive by night

Their goal, as always, to put out the light

To see the cogs in Life's great machine

Grind to a halt, now silent and mean

To long for peace, yet not willing to defend

What kind of message will that send?

Neither resignation nor defeat must carry the day

So one must rise again, each and every day

Life too can be fragile if denied by all

With no caring what is there to block the fall

If no one stands up for what is right

Beware then the fast approaching night

The essence of how one walks in the world

With a resounding "NO" it answers, defiantly hurled

The pump may waken from its despair

When enough have proven they do care

Yet can even the light exhaust its primal source

Provoke a rupture worse than divorce

No arbitration or settlement can be found

The ship of Life will have simply run aground

The prospect of such an end of time

Should frighten every soul as it has mine

Life's children, Hope and Care

Must stay with the One to well fare

And what of adults who can face the same depletion

Be it due to some slow leak or massive conflagration

No different, though some innocence be lost

Guarding with vigilance, keep the truth at all cost

For multiple times will one go to the mat

Even if the truth seems clear and pat

Evil too fights to carry the day

Though it be night, and forever stay

To lose faith in another, must it surely bring?

Some wound deep and profound with its painful sting

How many times can one bounce back?

Before there appears a fatal crack

Where, in place of a helping hand to extend

One whose sole desire is to heal and mend

Suspicion takes the place of kind

A sure sign of an altered mind

There is then the matter of why one was chosen

What determines who will touch you before you have
frozen?

For in the other there is something we see

Or rather blind nowadays, we call it chemistry

We speak of balance, the ebb and flow of extremes

One part concrete, the other composed of dreams

The former inhabits us, the means to relate

Mundane things seen and dealt with, squarely on one's
plate

The other piece is the one that was never there

To see it alive and well in another, we can only care

For if it cannot be ourselves, what better way

Than to participate through another every day

A metaphorical solution to a problem that's real

Yet it's the key to just how deeply – and blindly – we feel

Was it ever designed to be more than a starting line?

The attraction not to be understood, to do so would malig

Its power derived from opposites that attract

Reason goes out the window and we act

Sadly these mystical illusions evaporate over time

Perhaps the charges neutralize each other, both yours and mine

And here must begin a process new

One forgotten by most, recalled but by a few

Passion to lust. Lust to care

Step into a new world, if you dare

This can occur time and again

It has to me, and I've reached for my pen

After it's gone and calm has returned

And the seared heart, so painfully burned

Returns to its natural state, alone yet caught

Able to think what experience has bought

Clarity comes at prices this high

As to the truth we draw even more nigh

The mystery solidifies under reason's gaze

No longer can we live in some perpetual haze

And with each successive event of the heart

If we've played our cards well and assumed our part

Pain devolves into banality as scars take form

The badges of healing, not often proudly worn

What's happened to that original heart – soft, supple and pure?

Through all of the trials it was forced to endure

Has it grown hard, calloused and deformed?

Has its vocation been altered, its essence suborned?

How many blows must it suffer?

Can wisdom provide a useful buffer

Will its vision see more greys than whites?-

Has it will enough to engage in still more fights?

For the soul of the other, now back to the start

What are the true ways of the heart?

There you have another mysterious end

It's not from ill will, if a clear answer I do not send

For I am in the middle, still finding my way

Sometimes deeply disheartened at what others have to say

Little interest, less care, even less awareness

Some days seem lived in isolation – I do confess

When did we lose the faculty to build towards hope?

When was the future banished, leaving us only to cope?

For the future must function like a universal magnet

Drawing us towards her, a clear objective set

A new day has come after a night of disillusion

Where those I care for left me in confusion?

Where all only wanted to have their say

Wasting precious time so early in the day

Seizing a conversation as if Attila the Hun

Putting a good face on and speaking of their fun

But never a nod is given to any true complaint

As the hosts of heaven and every single saint

Were watching over us, so happy we can be

Blindness in all its form, a true miracle to see

I assemble my forces, those that remain

I go down by the river to wash out the night's stain

I seem to reemerge, discouragement's centripetal force

Has lost some of its strength, so today there will be no
divorce

That new door, the new beginning, that which I seek

I seem to hope it is there while waiting for a peek

Life needs a purpose, we search, but do we ever find?

Holding fast to our essence – innocent, hopeful and
where still appropriate, always kind

So back to the trenches, no idea where to go

I wonder if I find it, how will I know?

Or each night like some mechanical watch I must wind

For whatever reason, has it become no more than a
grind?

If that were to be, how would we live?

If we are here to nurture and give

Perhaps if we abandon the light, will frustration take hold?

With primal urges and a heart so cold

Some have simplified it, others set it apart

In the mix have they not lost their heart?

But what else is there, this tool divine?

Which determines in the end which road is mine.

Go dark if you feel drawn to its lies

Watch only the ground while denying the skies

Forget that though born of the mud, we can rise

To things that exist if we but use our eyes

To have is the now, the concrete, the real

Eat. Sleep. Hunt for the next meal

Living like this, every day will be the same

Devoid of what makes everything special – is that your game?

Or lift your eyes up to the heavens

Roll the dice for those lucky sevens

Dare to dream of things that don't yet exist

Hold fast to the future, don't ever desist.

CALLA LILIES

November 2017

Starting with Volume I, some of you may have followed my journey of grieving for my Lily. It has been three years, and nothing seemed to diminish what I felt having cared for her during her last four months, clinging to hope that the 50/50 chance they gave her would land her on the right side. She tried her best, against impossible odds, fighting until the very last, for me, until she couldn't anymore. And still she fought. But that last night, Death himself had to come and take her away. I saw him and will never forget how he sucked the life from her. But before he did, I thanked her for all the love she gave me, for her courage, her dignity, her selflessness, when we greater creatures would have taken the easy way out. So I told her she could go. And she was no more. In spite of all I did, I felt I had failed, for it was my purpose to keep her safe. Months later, when visiting my daughter and her family in Italy, I found myself at Ikea furniture shopping with my daughter. Quite by chance, in the plants section (always a favorite of mine), I saw dozens of Calla Lilies. I bought one for my daughter, entrusting it to her care, and not just the plant, but also the memory. And I ordered some bulbs online. I planted them on my return, and have watched them grow and thrive, living in my home. They are seasonal plants with a relatively short flowering season. It has been months now, and my "Lily" flowers still.. For once again, I have a Lily in my life, and it seems to hurt less fo now I have a Lily to care for. Like Persephone, she will bloom again each spring – it's not a lot. But it is something.

It's been many months and the pain remains

Fading with time, like laundry stains

Never to be forgotten or disappear

There are many times I feel you near

Memories dissolve slowly into the mist

And I indulge in remembering, I can't resist

Yet I have found a lighter way

To keep my promise and have you stay

When Death decided otherwise

It's a failure each time that open it pries

When last in Rome, a family trip

By chance I came across a flower I could not skip

Ikea's bounty gave me a thought

A solution to keep you somehow alive I bought

I searched online, a provider I found

And several bulbs of Calla Lilies were homeward bound

I bought the dirt, and found the pots

I planted the bulbs – for there were lots

And now they've grown, their blooms live

I tend to you through them, with the love I give

My heart cries less often, not every day

I no longer mourn in the same way

And each time I see your blooms at home

You aren't gone foreve, I no longer feel so alone.

FAITH MEETS HOPE

June 2017

Faith and Hope, along with a few other essentials of our lives can become harder to find. They are vital, for they allow us to transcend a reality which will never lack for challenges. But what force in the universe supports them for few things can come from nothing? As you will see, perhaps I didn't provide THE answer. But hopefully, in reading, you will think yourself, and quite possibly it will be you who find the answer. And if you do, please don't hesitate to share it.

You think to control your heart and freeze it cold

When it only makes you prematurely old

Cynics - those embracing hope that's lost

By life have been too often tossed

But something survives buried within you deep

The hill to climb looks now perhaps too steep

But here I am, a hand always there

You know you can, you must dare

Revive those dreams, feel the rush they provide

Step into the sunshine, you no longer need hide

Your shackles of dark illusions, aside them cast
They have no place in the future, but in your past

A new voice, in tune with your heart's current pace
Though much time seems wasted, this is not some race
But a quest, your salvation, the one you seek
The one that frightened you when allowed a first peek

Too close to your truth did it come?
Too high a hill to climb on the run?
Forgetting even where you are
Everything seemed much too far

It all depends on how one sees these things
Only children need to believe they can grow wings
To fly to the top, no effort required
As long as you breathe, by dreams be inspired

--

Think back to days when to survive each day was the goal

To avoid starvation, and by fate not be swallowed whole

Too many things we take for granted

There are always new ideas waiting to be planted

We've mastered life through civilization

Created a secure state, built a nation

Insulating us from Life's golden rule

Perfection as a goal? Impossible and cruel.

If I cannot be king of the world

If flags are raised, toes are curled

When I walk by, to be admired

Will I come crashing down when fired?

Stimulation, excitement, love, fun

Pleasures devoured on the run

The world on its head, you chose dark over light
And put down your arms before you began to fight

Faith needs hope to survive
Eyes but on the latter will bury the former alive
These are matters where logic holds little sway
Emotions see more clearly, they point the way

When doubt leads to fear, fear abandons love
Yet when needed, like to Noah, comes the dove
Soft and gentle, not harsh or filled with hate
Bringing back into focus the next gate

Not the final one, for always another appears
To challenge once again across the years
A final peace comes but at the end
When no more challenges does Life send

Will courage always come to save the day?

Will there never be a price to pay?

Of course, no valued thing comes for free

We buy our freedom from slavery

Not one imposed by evil men

Not even some angry God who strikes when

We are weakest, as if to say

Your will counts for naught, He will have his way

For born with resources rarely recognized

When needed they can be realized

Others shape them, wanting them resized

No constance exists as to what is prized

Life's circle where hope emerges giving birth to faith

Will the angel appear or the ancient wraith

What is that thing that will get you over the line?

And will it arrive just in time?

Imperfect, unsure, future is an uncharted land

Yet be certain of the unfailing, caring, offered hand

Will it be taken, is the time now right?

Or does darkness still obscure the light?

All I know is what I've said

Seeds herein planted once they are read-

This is the way I know how to do

This is my way, tried and true

This is the way, my part I fulfill

This is the way, embrace the drill

Step into Life's rhythm, you've been out of synch

And here's I'll stop – thank God – out of ink.

DON QUIXOTE 2018

January 2018

Most everyone knows the story of Don Quixote, the old fool who saw beauty where everyone else so what was real. In that vision, he found nobility, no matter how hidden it was by vulgar exteriors. And in so doing, he inspired those to whom he revealed their own inner beauty. They were inspired to live the nobility that had been revealed to them. It was a wonderful antidote to the cynicism, the realism that can poison an existence. Seeing not only what is but what might be in people is not just a gift. It is something we so badly need to be reminded of. All things considered, who was the fool?

Imagine a hero long ago written

One we all know and have been smitten

By his many seemingly contrary traits

His destiny determined by the fates

By what he saw in the world observed

Noblility and beauty well deserved

Yet alone was he to see such things

No matter, he had the heart of kings

How to explain the enigma that was he

Was he a slave or was he free?

What was it that this vision enabled?

His story to this day, still fabled

A choice,it seems, one made by him

A purity of heart, devoid of sin

To stand and fight, no chance to win

Not for land, or wealth, or vengeance of kin

Touching those he met along the way

Speaking of matters unusual for the day

Was he mocking their meager circumstance?

Better to boast and lead the dance

For the world had lost what he had found

Their resonance made a foreign sound

No reward was there for his noble cause

No right or wrong by mankind's laws

No hesitation, his heart knew when right

Courage flowed freely, knowing no fright

Did it truly matter if he won or lost?

Even if his life should be the cost?

Mocked by most who saw only a fool

Who was this old madman,was he someone's tool?

In the end, lost or found? He passed away

Though no stranger to doubt, he did not sway

Such is what comes when one is clear

When heart and mind join together, near

To know the truth of what does count

Not for sale or loan for any amount

A hero, yes, of the kind too rarely seen

Could he exist today in this world grown mean?

Can light survive the struggle with darkness?

Will it grown dim, illuminating less?

Weakened by compromise. Pragmatism required

In complications and absolutes mired?

There is no answer, universal, good for all

Each has a choice, to rise or fall

To find the reason and the strength to resis

To look evil in the eye and raise a fist

Or say "No matter," and lose it all

Into the shadows forever to fall

We have but one example, neither simple nor clear

Knowing only he was sure and knew no fear

To live in the sun, not the safety of shadows

A difficult matter. – An open road or one that narrows?

Don Quixote lives in each of us in some small way

We can enhance his light each and every day

To seek the good, beauty, and all that's pure

Suffer the setbacks with courage, resist and endure

Finding purpose and peace in life, seeing it unfold

Abandon the challenge and our souls are sold

Why do the young so fear to be bold?

In this search for glory and gold

After all, that's what they've been told

What is its true worth, this metal cold?

Could the time have come that hand to fold?

Look inside, let is speak, your life remold

To grow up for real, renewed, maybe even grow old?

To become more truly yourself; a thought to ponder and hold.

FINITE
January 2018

The first time I remember hearing this term evoked in a political sense was back in the 1970's when Jerry Brown was first governor of California. At the time, his was a solitary voice in trying to awaken us from the intoxicated state we were living in. The Seventies were not a happy time, and were possibly one of the decades when the infamous American Dream was in danger of losing its luster. The message was simple. Nothing should ever be taken for granted when it comes to Nature, in particular. Water is finite, clean air is finite, arable land is finite, and the human population is a matter of simple space correleated to our numbers – ignoring distribution. At that time, there were the beginnings of some concern about overpopulation. But with the Eighties came a resurgent economy worldwide, and the forgetfulness of prosperity reclaimed us. Nothing has changed since then, in spite of the financial crisis, certain technological improvements, and the dead end the debate around Climate Change has become. In fact, as I point out in

The world is a finite place

Something which has escaped the human race

We rush ahead, growth the goal

With no concern for the eventual toll

What happened to our capacity to thin

Has it been drowned in the kook aide we drink

There was a time when our most precious wish

Was to leave to our children oceans filled with fish

Not to feed our avide appetites

But to marvel at nature's bounty in our sites

To breathe an air devoid of risk

Preferring an air that clean and brisk

And the water, the most important for all that lives

Imagine a world where foul smells and toxins are what it gives

The land which welcomed us when we left the muck

Why poison what sustains us - honestly what the fuck?

It seems we have reached a point of no return

Our bridges to the future we choose to burn

In so doing the gap between then and now

Will continue to shrink if we allow

The hole in our souls that we don't see

The one that drives all forms of avidity

That empty our hearts, leaving us hungry

Can have but one finality

The meal will end, it must when all is consumed

When that day arrives, we will have ourselves doomed

No talk of God – empty prayers of the devout

To continue down this road proves beyond a doubt

That we have forgotten what the words are about

Empty words with any God can carry no clout

Repeated so often, the mind needs not mean each line

No one would notice the insincerity so it should be fine

What does it mean to be present as the words are said?

Do we ponder each time, or are they dead?

Prayer are reminders, so we don't forget their role

Willfully busy , we forget the need to become more whole

This is why, if a reason truly exists

We were put here to progress, not raise our fists

If life has become something learned by rote

All one has to do is repeat and quote

If God there is, would he not see?

These supplications miss the point entirely

There may be suffering as deep as the ocean

Passions may rise, but what of emotion?

Slavish conformity – is that really devotion?

Without sincerity, no caring, there is no magic potion

So there we are, the end of the road?

It has been a long journey, time to lay down the load?

We either find a way forward, to progress

To learn to live more and consume less

Ease and comfort, plenty, the absence of need

Ironically engender only selfishness and greed

Where is the joy one can find in the gift?

Have we lost the ability to feel the lift?

That can come when our core is revealed

When without fear or ambivalence it can be revealed

When our souls have been healed

Perhaps then our fate can be unsealed

Why hide when we have been so blessed?

If we have all we need, why still hunger for the rest?

If indeed we continue and before and miss the turn

If our future we continue to burn?

If we have reached the end of time

Say simply to yourself, the fault was mine

MAKE AMERICA GREAT AGAIN

January 2017

I made no selection in terms of which rhyme would close this collection. I did want to end on a positive note. But current events – February 2018 – would not allow it. And in the spirit of the title – The Prophet – it would not have been consistent to end on some naïve optimist note. Like all the poems here, my purpose was never to approve or condemn any fact. My hope was that by putting up something of a more future – and not present – oriented mirror, was might all come to recognize that the path we are on will most certainly not take us to where we want to go. But as we all have a voice, we all have a voice. And the choice to whether or not, and how, to use it, belongs to each of us. The final outcome depends on that, and that alone. There can be no one else to blame.

The title, a phrase often stated, rarely understood

Supposedly evoking past days when things were good

Ask someone who has placed this phrase

In his discourse on too many days

When exactly did these good times prevail?

And if they were so good, how did we fail?

To ensure they would last longer than they did

Were they childhood memories back when but a kid

When parents saw to every need

The only requirement, their words to heed

Or perhaps from a time, when as adults starting out

When responsibilities were something rarely thought about

Then there was the time when the children were young

When all thoughts turned to their well being and the time spent among

When they thought less about their own frustrations, normal in life

Whether they came from children, work, husband or wife

And now that they're older, alone and with times on their hands

To feel lost and useless, preoccupations becoming demands

Not of themselves, from the time when they took care of things

With the satisfaction providing most often brings

These times are dangerous, for thoughts turn inward, feelings somehow passed by

Too much time on their hands, though they could always ask why

Of themselves, for all the things left undone

For good and bad reasons, unfinished business calls, frustration begun

Prosperity comes in waves, like the oceans blue

And so do storms, so what should one do?

Without one the other would grow unbearably same

And neither could we grow nor understand the game

One things is certain, time will always grow short

As life slips through our fingers, hope begins to abort

The gap separating present and future begins to shrink

If we've spent our lives too busy, and forgotten how to think

With pleasures indulged, selfishness grew

The world has shrunk, and it's now all about guess who

Like children we complain, no ownership do we feel

Complaints grow unreasonable, crowds form and begin to squeal

Reason dissolves in a flood of resentment

Without wisdom there can be neither peace nor contentment

So when you hear the roar of praise for false prophets who claim

The good old days can be had again, write down their name

Think back not only to when but also to why

Were those good old days really that good – go ahead and try

Don't be afraid to acknowledge mistakes

Those who deny them are nothing but fakes

How else do we learn but through bridges we burn?

Childhood issues that endure, and our emotions churn

Isn't it time to let go of those filters, and start again to learn?

That life is neither fair, nor honest nor good at each turn

We all got our share of good times and bad?

There is no one in charge, so don't be so mad

Look to yourself, it's all you control

Life is a highway and there is always a toll

Time never forgives, nor does it forget

Life is all about jumping in and getting wet

If things don't turn out the way you had planned

Don't look to others, something better to demand

Fair is not something to which Nature subscribes

It responds neither to punishments, complaints or bribes

Hope exists to transcend the days that are tough

Life rarely burdens us with too much – mostly enough

If challenged we are, it's a chance to know

First, that we will reap whatever we sow

Second, circumstance often escapes our control

Third, no one gets more than a piece of the whole

So cry if indeed that's what you prefer

Know beforehand it will only deter

For wishes are the stuff of dreams

Never worth much more than any hill of beans

Value resides in what you yourself have done

There was joy, there was pain, but the race was run

It's how you ran, did you do your best?

Only then can you know if you passed the test.

You alone can judge, no other can know

Did you honor Life, did you grow?

Were you there when needed or did you turn away?

When Life called out to you, what did you say?

Did you cheer or did you cry?

Did you make believe or did you try?

Did you know how little value there is in the things you buy?

But most of all, did you always ask yourself why?

This perhaps is the true American Dream

Not some fantasy we try and keep squeaky clean

Look at who we have become of late

There is your answer to what will be our fate

For more information:

www.analticalpsychologynyc.com

or write

analyticalpsychologynyc@gmail.com

ABOUT THE AUTHOR

The Unlikely Poet

Mitchell Ritter is a native New Yorker, born and raised in Brooklyn. He left for Europe after graduating from Colgate University to enter a Clinical Psychology Program at the Universite de Geneve, Switzerland, where the emphasis was on primarily on cognitive development in children (J. Piaget). In parallel, he studied at the C. G. Jung Institute for Analytical Psychology, Zurich and Kussnacht. Working in an outpatient clinic and in private practice for over 10 years before entering the private sector in a variety of functions with several major multinational companies. During this period he maintained a private practice as well.

Father of two wonderful daughters, now grown and parents themselves, he returned to his native New York in 2002. He worked in a number of marketing practices where his scientific background and interests established him as a valued player.

During these years, he also maintained a private practice , now located on the Upper East Side in Manhattan.

An avid tennis player, dog owner, his latest incarnation as a "rhymer" in the Seussian tradition (always a source of disarming wisdom} came out of the blue. A strong believer in Life, opportunities often arrive that way. In fact, the more one accepts them when offered, the more frequently they arrive. Always living in at least two worlds simultaneously, a native curiosity, a caring nature, and a certain intelligence make his lines always questioning, at times disturbing, but fundamentally hopeful, convinced that we are put here for a reason, our role being to find that North Star which points the way foward. He recommends readers approach these rhymes as if they were *Tappas*, intellectual appetizers. Let yourself be tempted by what calls out to you. Consume the lines with savor, and when finished, you may also have found food for thought – simple looking yet complex, plainly spoken yet nuanced, personal yet universal - and maybe even some nourishment for the soul.

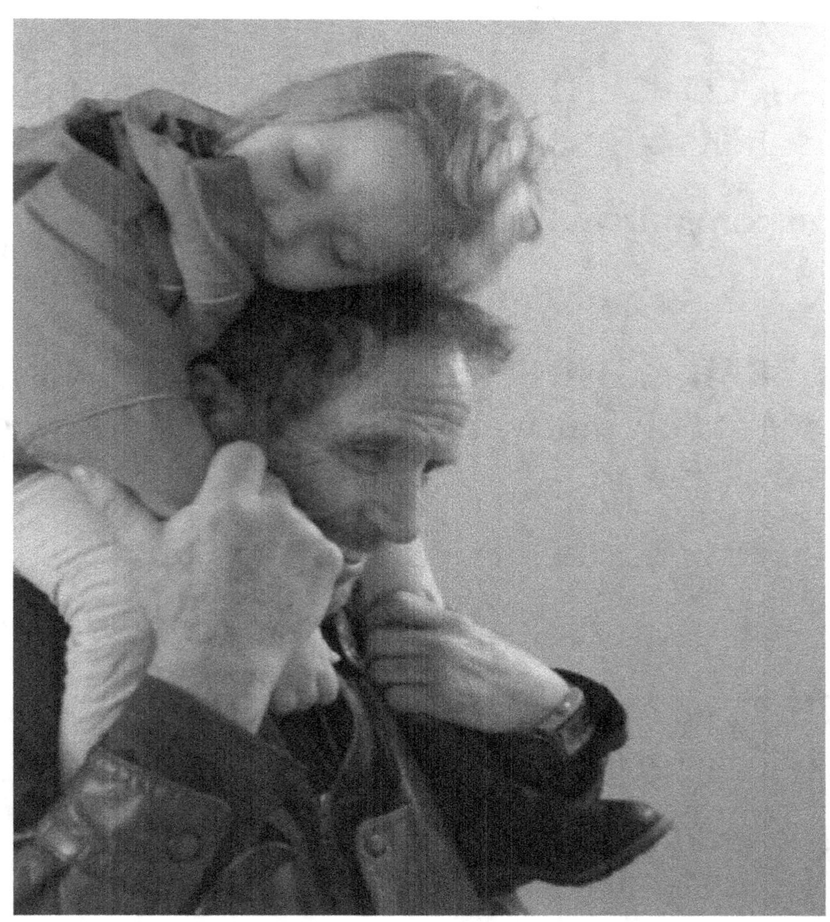

ALSO AVAILABLE FROM

THE AUTHOR

MR. HIDE'S PROGRESS* – a short story about why people make the wrong choices, is available on

WWW.Amazon.com/mitcellritter/MRHIDESPROGRESS

www.createspace.com/**6876165**

SIX YEARS – A CONCENTRATE OF LIFE* – the first phase of the author coming home after half a lifetime away

www.amazon.com/mitchell ritter/ebooks/SIX EARS

www.createspace.com/**6876165**

***IN THE 7TH YEAR – THE FUTURE IS WAITING–** Phase II and taking note of just how much American culture had moved on from the 1970's, is available on

www.Amazon.com/mitchellritter /INTHE7THYEAR

www.createspace.com/**7888004**

THE PROPHET* – Dead Ends and Other Perils – A look at the road we are on, where it will take us from the heart,

www.amazon.com/mitchellritter/the **Prophet**

www.createspace.com/**7189577**

*AVAILABLE IN *EBOOK* OR SOFT COVER FORMATS